That
Self-Forgetful
Perfectly Useless
Concentration

THAT

~~Self-Forgetful~~

Perfectly Useless

»Concentration«

ALAN
SHAPIRO

The University of Chicago Press
Chicago and London

Alan Shapiro is the William R. Kenan Jr. Distinguished Professor of English at the University of North Carolina at Chapel Hill. A member of the American Academy of Arts and Sciences, he has published many books of poetry, including the National Book Award finalist *Night of the Republic* and the Pulitzer Prize finalist *Reel to Reel*; translations, *Trojan Women* and *The Oresteia*; two memoirs, *The Last Happy Occasion* and *Vigil*; and the novel *Broadway Baby*. A new book of poems, *Life Pig*, is also available from the University of Chicago Press.

The University of Chicago Press, Chicago 60637
The University of Chicago Press, Ltd., London
© 2016 by The University of Chicago
All rights reserved. Published 2016.
Printed in the United States of America

25 24 23 22 21 20 19 18 17 16   1 2 3 4 5

ISBN-13: 978-0-226-41681-6 (cloth)
ISBN-13: 978-0-226-41695-3 (paper)
ISBN-13: 978-0-226-41700-4 (e-book)
DOI: 10.7208/chicago/9780226417004.001.0001

Library of Congress Cataloging-in-Publication Data
Names: Shapiro, Alan, 1952– author.
Title: That self-forgetful perfectly useless concentration / Alan Shapiro.
Description: Chicago : The University of Chicago Press, 2016.
Identifiers: LCCN 2016019568 | ISBN 9780226416816 (cloth : alk. paper) | ISBN 9780226416953 (pbk. : alk. paper) | ISBN 9780226417004 (e-book)
Subjects: LCSH: Shapiro, Alan, 1952– | Poetry.
Classification: LCC PS3569.H338 Z46 2016 | DDC 811/.54 [B] —dc23 LC record available at https://lccn.loc.gov/2016019568

♾ This paper meets the requirements of ANSI/NISO Z39.48-1992 (Permanence of Paper).

Contents

Convention and Self-Expression

1

In 1965, in a bookstore in my hometown of Brookline, Massachusetts, in the late afternoon of an ordinary schoolday, in the middle of winter, I discovered my inner nonconformist. Anyone who might have seen me standing before the tiny poetry section, turning the pages of Lawrence Ferlinghetti's *A Coney Island of the Mind*, would have mistaken me for an unremarkable thirteen-year-old in a winter coat, unbuckled galoshes, a book bag slung over his shoulder. And up to that moment that's exactly who I was, a typical middle-class Jewish kid whose parents worked long hours for little pay, with three kids and my mother's mother to care for. Life in the household was always sulky at the best of times, and now and then explosive. Terrified of blow-ups, I did my best to fit in. I did my best to be the kind of kid my parents expected me to be. I kept my hair cut short, I dressed neatly; I worked hard in school. I seldom got into trouble. I was more angster than gangster—the only tough guys I ever dreamed of being were the Jets and Sharks in the film version of the musical *West Side Story*, which I had seen with a few friends the year before. When the movie let out, my friends and I went dancing down the street looking for Puerto Ricans to beat up. The gang dissolved later the same day when I picked a fight with Michael Lee, a bespectacled diminutive Chinese boy, the closest thing my neighborhood had to a Puerto Rican. Unfortunately, Mike Lee fought like Bruce Lee's little brother, and I was crying uncle after the first punch landed.

But reading Ferlinghetti, I entered an alternate universe that turned on its head the world of my parents: its holy trinity of rank commercialism, status seeking, and sexual prudery. Ferlinghetti denounced American consumerism "singing from the Yellow Pages." Unlike my elders, he wanted to be a "social climber climbing downward." In his smart-alecky way, he counseled us to "confound the system," "to empty our pockets," "to miss our appointments," to leave "our neckties behind . . . and take up the full beard of walking anarchy."

Longings I didn't know I had suddenly sprang to life: mine was the heart Ferlinghetti described as a foolish fish cast up and gasping for love "in a blather of asphalt and delay." I wanted to be robust, uninhibited, and wide open to the world like the dog trotting "freely in the street . . . touching and tasting and testing everything." I thrilled to Ferlinghetti's advocacy of contrarianism for its own sake, as if it were a badge of authenticity or the height of courage to walk out into traffic when the Don't Walk sign was flashing.

When I left the store, I may still have been that middle-class kid, diffident, self-conscious, and too eager to please. But from then on I was inwardly transformed. I lived a secret life in the poetry I went on to read, and in the poems I began to write. On the page I undermined the rules I lived by off the page. I dreamed of the world Ferlinghetti invited me to enter, a world of impulse and imagination where lovers went "nude in the profound lasciviousness of spring in an algebra of lyricism." What Ferlinghetti offered was a state of mind nearly everyone my age had begun imagining, each of us planning our great escape to what he called the Isle of Manisfree, where we could do our own thing in exactly the same way.

2
―

Flash forward to the summer of 1970. I'm eighteen years old. It's a Friday night and I'm getting ready to go out with my girlfriend Martha. I'm five-feet-eight-and-three-quarter-inches tall, but between my long thick curly blond hair frizzing out in all directions and my thick-heeled black shit-kicker boots, I'm closer to six feet. I'm six feet tall and I've got a nickel bag of pot in a front pocket of my yellow bell-bottoms. That's right, yellow bell-bottoms. Which is to say, I'm feeling pretty good. I'm one of the hip, truly liberated people. Liberated but not stupid, which is why I've told my parents that I'll be sleeping over at a friend's house when in fact I'll be driving with Martha to Rockport, where we'll sneak into an empty summer house her parents own and spend the entire night together, for one night at least not having to d-d-d-do it in the road.

On the way out of the house I pass the wall of family photographs: grandparents, parents, aunts, and uncles. In the largest one, a black-and-white picture of my father's family taken at a Boston restaurant just after the war: my father's brother and sister-in-law and two of his older sisters and their husbands sit at a table while a third sister and her husband, plus my parents and grandparents, stand behind them. The table is round, and there's a white carnation in the middle of it surrounded by empty plates, drinks, water glasses, and the crumpled napkins of those who have had to stand for the picture. Everyone is smiling out at the photographer.

My father wears a dark double-breasted suit with wide lapels, the knot of his fat tie is loosened, and his fedora is tipped back in a way he no doubt thinks is both casual and chic, a Jewish Frank Sinatra; my mother wears a pale evening gown with a pointed bust, small waist, and rounded shoulder line. Her hair is marcelled in a thick wave that gathers without breaking down the right side of her face. The other women all have perms, and between their gloved fingers they hold cigarettes that burn at the end of elegantly long and slender holders.

It's just after the war, and though my father still works long hours for little pay in the slaughterhouse his older brother and his father own, he plans to go into business for himself once he saves a little money. My mother is soon to be pregnant. She herself is the product of a broken home, an unfortunate marriage. Raised by her grandparents, she is determined to be a perfect wife, a perfect mother, to give her future children the childhood she never had. She is certain she will love them with a vengeance.

In 1970, though, none of this is really visible to me. My parents, newly married in the photo, look out at the camera, both only a few years older than I am now as I stare up at them, utterly astonished by the thought. Young as their faces seem, young and hopeful, everyone smiling out at the camera as if no one could ever be as happy as they were at that moment, I don't believe it, not for a second. I don't believe they were ever really young, not young like I am young. I mean, look at them, look at their clothes, their formal ties and jackets, their cuffs, their watches, the dainty gloves, all the conventional trappings of an old-world dream of success and status seeking. Surely they must have seen how antiquated and frumpy it all was, even then, when they were new to it—the black-and-white motion pictures, the corny dialogue ("aw, that'll be swell, kid," "ah, you big lug"), the shaky newsreels, the crackly recordings of big band music, and the ancient crooners, and the songs, my God, the songs, the cornball lyrics ("in a mountain greenery where God paints the scenery"—are you kidding me?)—even then they must have seen how goofily drenched in oldness their lives were, drenched in the conventions, formalities, customs, and lingo of a culture my generation has had the good sense to abandon.

My generation, talking about my generation, what does style have to do with us; we transcend style; we reject all notions of style, of lifestyles, that awful word, in favor of what if not sheer life itself. We worship at the altar of the natural, the unadorned, the uninhibited. Thank God, I think, I was born when I was and live when I do. In the eternal present uncontaminated by the uptight past.

I turn my back on the gone world of my elders. As I step outside, easily six feet two by now, maybe even taller, I discover I already know the words to "In the Summertime," the new hit single by Mungo Jerry. I think Mungo Jerry is the name of the lead singer of the band, not the name of the band itself, a name which the lead singer, Paul Dorset, had adopted from T. S. Eliot's *Old Possum's Book of Practical Cats*. But I don't know this yet. I don't even know they're British. And as far as T. S. Eliot goes, well, I haven't read a word he's written; in fact, I know of him only because he's mentioned along with Ezra Pound in Bob Dylan's "Desolation Row," a song I don't understand but have memorized anyway because Dylan is a genius, my generation's

William Shakespeare, whom I'm not ashamed to say I also haven't read, though on a high school outing a few years back I did see the film version of *Romeo and Juliet*. What's Shakespeare to me? Or Eliot for that matter. I have long hair, yellow bell-bottoms, and a bag of pot in my front pocket. My passionate rejection of class and status notwithstanding, I'm sitting proudly behind the wheel of my father's 1963 big-finned Buick Le Sabre, and as I drive away I sing, too young and too full of life for irony, "If her daddy's rich, take her out for a meal, / if her father's poor, just do what you feel . . ." "In the summertime when the weather is high, / you can stretch right up and touch the sky, / when the weather's fine, you got women, you've got women on your mind, / have a drink have a drive, go out and see what you can find."

3

In 1974, one of my mother's contemporaries, the British poet Philip Larkin, brought out his last full-length volume of poetry, *High Windows*. I didn't read the book till 1975, after I had moved to Dublin to live a writer's life, which at the time meant getting as far away as possible from my parents and everything associated with my past.

I remember coming across *High Windows* in a small bookstore off Grafton Street, a few doors down from a restaurant called Captain America, where my new Irish girlfriend liked to eat because she found the food, the hamburgers and hotdogs, exotic. Odd to see myself back then in that tiny bookstore, half slumped, with my back against a bookshelf in a dimly lit aisle, head bent over the book, my long hair cascading down to the shoulders of my Aran sweater, as I read the title poem, not quite knowing what to make of it:

When I see a couple of kids
And guess he's fucking her and she's
Taking pills or wearing a diaphragm,
I know this is paradise

Everyone old has dreamed of all their lives—
Bonds and gestures pushed to one side
Like an outdated combine harvester,
And everyone young going down the long slide

To happiness, endlessly. I wonder if
Anyone looked at me forty years back,
And thought, *That'll be the life,*
No God anymore, or sweating in the dark

About hell and that, or having to hide
What you think of the priest. He
And his lot will all go down the long slide
like free bloody birds. And immediately

Rather than words, comes the thought of high windows:
The sun comprehending glass,
And beyond it, the deep blue air, that shows
Nothing, and is nowhere, and is endless.

Of course I liked the vulgar jokiness of the opening lines. But I was mystified by the turn the poem takes to an older world and its particular historically determined styles of inhibition and longing—no sweating in the dark about hell, or having to hide what you think of the priest? So far as I knew my parents and grandparents cared about God and religion about as little as they cared about pleasure. It had never occurred to me to think they envied anything about me or my generation. They held our vision of freedom in complete contempt. So shackled by the mores and conventions of their time, they didn't have the sense to know what actual freedom was. Their idea of the good life was to work themselves sick to have a little extra for a sick day. At least that's how I saw it then.

I bristled at the thought that each generation of the middle-aged and elderly projects onto the generation after them all of their unrealized desires, that my passionate intensity could ever be like theirs or anyone else's in any way, or that the optimism of the young of every generation embodied only the typical upside of an eternally recurring cycle of delusion and disenchantment. I resisted the assumption that each generation has its own historically contingent modes of thinking and feeling, its own particular conventions to which familiarity bred of habit gives a veneer of inevitability. And the closing lines, what could I make of them, the elevated diction, the metaphysical imagery, or the solemn yet ironic evocation of the blank, limitless blue air of desire whose intensity increases the more unfulfillable it is? If by 1975 I didn't feel all that happy or free, despite the romance of the move to Ireland, despite my Irish girlfriend, that was only because I hadn't yet completely exorcised the vestiges of my upbringing, though with every ounce of vital energy inside me I was certain that I soon would. I could no more think of the values I espoused as someday becoming obsolete than I could imagine bell-bottoms being anything but cool, or a Mustang or Corvette someday looking just as laughably old-fashioned as an Edsel or a Rambler.

Mostly, I balked at what the poem seemed to say: that what I and my fellow travelers in the counter culture thought of as 20-20 vision was only generational myopia. I couldn't accept the poem, but I couldn't forget it either.

4

The monthly calendar pages flutter up and away one after another till it's 1976 or '77, 11:00 on a Thursday morning, and I'm sitting in Donald Davie's office at Stanford University, discussing Philip Larkin. Davie is a dark-suited, fifty-something, well-known and well-respected English poet-critic. Jovial, exuberant, incredibly learned, and wickedly articulate about what he loves and hates, a passionate enemy of groupthink yet politically conservative, a hardboiled Calvinist yet artistically open minded, even cosmopolitan, a lover of Thomas Hardy and Ezra Pound, Yvor Winters and George Oppen, the postmodern French poet Edmond Jabès and the American maverick Ed Dorn, to name only a few of the heterogeneous and contradictory poets he champions, he has pulled out four beers from the side drawer of his desk, two for me, two for him, and we drink while Davie describes the mental tightrope one has to walk in order to read poetry with any sort of seriousness and sensitivity. He tells me that every way of writing entails a bias, every stylistic choice directs attention to this instead of that, encourages implicit or explicit agreement or dissent. But to let a work's moral or political bias blind you to its aesthetic value is as limiting as to let its aesthetic value blind you to its moral bias. With someone like Pound, for instance, you can't appreciate the poetry without anguish because you can't disentangle its aesthetic achievement from its political affiliations; to do so would be to trivialize both.

So, I say, what about Larkin, what do you make of Larkin? Davie doesn't like Larkin's little Englandism, his provincial narrow-minded dismissal, on and off the page, of modernism and internationalism. He finds Larkin's defense of ordinariness, his debunking of what Davie calls all sense of the marvelous and strange, a failure of nerve and a stultifying retreat from contemporary life. At the same time, Davie says Larkin is a master of the lyric poem and isn't as old-fashioned or antiromantic as he pretends to be. His originality, Davie says, is indistinguishable from his conventionality, his fluency, so to speak, in the metrical and even romantic conventions he often appears to be debunking. Maybe it's the beer I've knocked back too quickly, but I'm confused by how Larkin could be considered original in any way whatsoever. His poems are too straightforward, too plain, too, I don't know, old-fashioned. What's original about "High Windows"?

Davie pulls off an anthology from the bookshelf behind him. He reads me the first couple of stanzas from the old ballad "Mary Hamilton," then a short tetrameter lyric, "Madam, withouten many words" by Sir Thomas Wyatt; then "A Valediction Forbidding Mourning" by John Donne and Marvell's "The Mower to the Glow-Worms." He puts the book down, grabs another book off the shelf. He reads "The Oxen" and "In Time of Breaking of Nations" by Thomas Hardy, then Auden's "As I Went Out One Evening," and finally a couple of other poems, "To Earthward" by Robert Frost and "The Owl" by Edward Thomas, both poems in quatrains. When he finishes, he says, See what I mean? I don't see what he means. I'm too drunk by now to see what he means. I'm focusing on his thick black-rimmed glasses to keep the room from spinning.

It's 11:30 in the morning and I'm blotto.

Then Davie holds up "High Windows," turning the book toward me. "Look," he says, "Look at the bloody quatrains, quatrains you see, rhymed quatrains, just like all the other poems, except it isn't like them, is it?" He interprets my blank look as asking, "How so?" and he tells me, a little annoyed at my obtuseness, Because Larkin's lines aren't regular, and neither are his rhymes. Don't I see how he's evoking the convention and upending it? When I just stare at him dumbfounded, he says, "The lines, dear boy, the lines modulate randomly from anapestic trimeter or tetrameter to an occasional pentameter." Then he goes on to describe how the rhymes too appear at first to fall haphazardly. In the first two quatrains only lines 2 and 4 rhyme, though "paradise," which rhymes partially with "she's," makes more of an audible rhyme with "lives" in the first line of quatrain 2.

Now Davie has walked around the desk and put the book in my lap. He points out how all four lines in the third quatrain are rhymed in the conventional *abab* pattern but the rhymes are only partial, if-life, back-dark; and then he orders me to notice how Larkin crosses that emergent but not fully articulated chiming with the internal rhyme of "endlessly," the last word of the poem's first sentence, and "me," in the following line. It's really only in the fourth quatrain that the rhymes are fully audible, and Larkin underscores that audibility by rhyming again internally but this time on a word in the last line of this quatrain with a word in the first line of the next. This heightened formality coincides with the final turn in the poem from the demotic idiom of the preceding lines to a higher, more traditional register, as if on the level of style and form alone Larkin were working backward through time toward a less ironic more romantically effusive summoning of desire.

"But of course he can't escape his moment, can he, Alan?" Davie says, quizzically watching me now over his reading classes, which have slid down to the tip of his nose. "Surely," he asks, "you see how the irony persists even where the rhetoric is most expansive?"

When I don't answer, trying to focus on the swimming page, he points out how Larkin keeps the quatrains open by running the sentence on from stanza to stanza and how the beautiful line break after "shows" in the penultimate line intensifies our expectation for a final revelation, which only makes the negatives of the last line more emphatically disappointing, as does the last line's falling trochaic meter and the final rhyme of the accented "glass" with the unaccented second syllable of "endless." The closure you expect from rhyme, he tells me, is both solicited and left unsatisfied, which of course is itself an enactment of what everything else in the poem, from the irregular line lengths to the open quatrains, has been telling us all along: that nothing will satisfy our desire for paradise, that our desire for what we can't have has no end.

"Another beer?" Davie asks, and he pulls two more out of the desk drawer. I have no memory of what he says next. He has divided, amoebalike, into two Donald Davies, and both are now speaking in some ancient tongue, Linear B or Hittite, I can't tell which.

5
‾

What makes a poet new and different? When we call someone original, what exactly do we mean? Until the mid-eighteenth century, the concept of originality referred not to something new, fresh, or novel but to something really old, as in ancestral. *Original* suggested not a venturing out into unexplored or hitherto undiscovered territory but a return to a lost beginning, a break from prevailing social practices that have grown overly refined or repressive, so as to return to an uncorrupted vital source. Revolutionaries in religion and in art often draw on this older meaning of the term to justify their opposition to the things they want to change. Thus early Reformation theologians claimed the new and simpler forms of worship they espoused represented not a rejection of Christianity but a resurrection of the faith as it was in the time of the church fathers, a return to the original church before inauthentic practices and rituals corrupted it. In the preface to *Lyrical Ballads*, Wordsworth justifies abandoning the desiccated habits of neoclassical decorum, the entrenched excessively artificial conventions of his day, in favor of the generality of nature articulated in and through a natural idiom, a language actually spoken by common folk outside the exclusive high-class drawing rooms of London.

Closer to home, think too of many postwar poets who abandoned what they called a too-cooked rhetorical style of composition in favor of a looser and simpler, more improvisatory mode of writing that drew from wells far below the too-enculturated ego, that reached beyond mere individual consciousness to the irrational, presocialized collective unconscious, and even deeper to prehuman levels of being untainted by the depredations of Western culture. And then there are the more recent postmodern revolutionaries, the Language poets who, through fragmentation and irony, attempt to liberate the undergraduate, if not the underprivileged, from the shackles of clarity— deconstructing the deceptively coherent surfaces of discourse and the illusions of meaning, the false or simplifying forms of narrative, down to mere language itself, language as it really is, in its "natural" state, meaning with all of its Derridean instabilities, contradictions, and ambiguities in full display, the jury-rigged poststructural machine, so to speak, inside the ghost of referentiality. Even the new formalists, those well-groomed insurrectionists who put the net back into tennis but forgot about the ball, justified their rejection of free verse in favor of rhyme and meter by appealing to our biological nature, if not to nature itself. The iamb, they claimed, is more natural than the merely artificial conventions of nontraditional verse because it echoes the beating of the human heart.

And what about those of us who constituted the antiwar youth movement of the late 1960s and early '70s? Where exactly did we think we were going if not, as Joni Mitchell sings in "Woodstock," "back to the Garden"?

During my time at Stanford, largely through Donald Davie's influence, I began to puzzle over the role that convention plays in our experience of the new. I began to think of originality less in terms of making something up ex nihilo than in terms of bringing together and integrating elements that until this act of making had been found only in isolation. I became more interested in idiosyncrasy, in other words, than in the more romantic concept of originality.

6

In the late Renaissance or early Reformation, it was not unusual for artists, writers, and intellectuals to challenge one another to outrageous feats of physical endurance. On a bet, Will Kemp, the best known actor of his day, danced from London to Norwich, a journey of 130 miles. It's not known what kind of dance he did, but it's fun to picture him doing the Charleston or the twist across the English countryside. Someone—his name, alas, has not survived—won a considerable sum of money by walking backward from London to Berwick. In 1589 Robert Carey won a wager of £2,000 for walking the same route in twelve days. In 1618 the 280-pound, forty-six-year-old poet/playwright Ben Jonson, one of the most famous writers in England, walked from London to Edinburgh after betting someone in the Mermaid Tavern that he could.

When Jonson arrived in Edinburgh nearly three months

after setting out, he stayed a few weeks with William Drum-
mond, Lord of Hawthornden, during which, it seems, he had
an unsuccessful dalliance with a young woman, which inspired
the following poem:

MY PICTURE LEFT IN SCOTLAND

I now think love is rather deaf than blind,
 For else it could not be
  That she,
  Whom I adore so much should so slight me
And cast my love behind,
I'm sure my language to her was as sweet,
 And every close did meet
 In sentence of as subtle feet
 As hath the youngest he
That sits in shadow of Apollo's tree.
  O, but my conscious fears,
  That fly my thoughts between,
  Tell me that she hath seen
 My hundred of gray hairs,
 Told seven and forty years,
Read so much waste as she cannot embrace
My mountain belly and my rocky face;
And all these through her eyes have stopped her ears.

The athletic grace of the poem, the way the long complex sentences leap so balletically from line to line, the rhymes falling
into place as if by accident, is obvious. What's less obvious is
the poem's fresh reworking of the conventions of courtly love,
in which the lover is young and handsome and the language
is florid. Jonson overturns these expectations by the realistic

description of himself as middle-aged and overweight, and by employing a lively but plain diction. He signals his unconventional take on a conventional situation in the opening line by altering the cliché "love is blind" to "love is deaf." The poem is, in fact, a send-up of the whole Neoplatonic tradition of courtly love, in which the eyes are windows to the soul and the mutable body is less important than immutable spirit. If these clichés were true, Jonson implies, then the beauty of his language should have been more than enough to win the girl's affection. But his all-too-mutable body got in the way ("And all these through her eyes have stopped her ears"). He invokes the tradition in order to show how divorced it is from actual life.

In a poem written roughly 340 years later, the American poet J. V. Cunningham echoes Jonson in order to define himself against the clichés and conventions of his own time and place. Even the title of the poem—"The Aged Lover Discourses in the Flat Style"—establishes the conventions the poem will define itself against: we associate Petrarchan sonnets with a florid style and elaborate figures of speech all celebrating idealized romance among the young, but Cunningham will give us a flat discourse, consistent with a less idealized picture of intimacy, involving not the young but the aged:

> There are, perhaps, whom passion gives a grace,
> Who fuse and part as dancers on the stage,
> But that is not for me, not at my age,
> Not with my bony shoulders and fat face.
> Yet in my clumsiness I found a place
> And use for passion: with it I ignore
> My gaucheries and yours, and feel no more
> The awkwardness of the absurd embrace.

It is a pact men make and seal in flesh,
To be so busy with their own desires
Their loves may be as busy with their own,
And not in union. Though the two enmesh
Like gears in motion, each with each conspires
To be at once together and alone.

Where the conventional love poem finds love along with inti-macy, sexual pleasure, and balletic grace, Cunningham finds isolation and clumsiness, the intimacy more conspiracy to maintain privacy in the company of someone else. The young fuse like dancers; the old enmesh like gears. And yet as in Jon-son's poem the handling of the form couldn't be more elegant, despite the flatness of the language. There's beauty here, a grim realistic beauty, but it's not the kind one normally encounters in more conventional celebrations of love, on or off the page. And yet how else does the poem convey its unique, idiosyncratic perspective except by playing it off against the conventions it both inherits and redefines? The two poems, written some 340 years apart, subscribe to the same general assumption that to rework the conventions and mores that the past bequeaths to us, we have to know the past. Both poets view tradition as an ongoing conversation/argument about the nature of tradi-tion, about what forms are usable and which in need of renewal, adjustment, or resistance. But you can't adjust or resist what you're not aware of.

And this maybe was the problem with my generation, at least back in the day when we all had hair: like the young of any period, though only more so, we were too much of our moment to be aware of our moment. Because of our history, we postwar, post–Cuban Missile Crisis, American baby boomers, children of the war in Southeast Asia, of the struggle for civil rights and the doomsday clock set at five minutes to midnight, of Woodstock and the draft, we felt unmoored not only from the past but from the future too. Don't make plans, our gurus told us, just clap your hands. Because we believed all bonds and gestures were artificial shackles that in the little time before the bomb went off we'd shrug off so as to forge our own "original" relation to the world, we couldn't see how much the bonds and gestures of our moment were determining nearly everything we said and did.

Here's a poem by Natalie Diaz, a young Native American poet, that does to the traditional form of the triolet (usually written in rhyme and meter) what Cunningham has done to the Petrarchan sonnet: she reinvents it in ways wholly distinct and novel, personal and representative. And in doing so, Diaz illustrates a fundamental truth about poetry in general, that all poems are Janus faced: they always look in two directions, outward at the world beyond the poem and inward to the history of the art itself, so as to conduct their own particular reckonings with language and with life. The poem, the first in a short sequence titled "Downhill Triolets," is called "Sisyphus and My Brother." To fully experience and appreciate what the poem is doing, one has to know that the triolet is a highly lyrical overdetermined eight-line poem with multiple repeating lines, usually in rhyme and meter; one also has to be familiar with Greek mythology, as well with the destructive codependencies that addiction carries in its wake:

> The phone rings—my brother was arrested again.
> Dad hangs up, gets his old blue Chevy going, and heads to
>   the police station.
> It's not the first time, it's not even the second.
> No one is surprised my brother was arrested again.

The guy fell on my knife was his one-phone-call explanation.
(*He stabbed a man five times in the back* is the official
accusation.)
My brother is arrested again and again. And again
our dad, our Sisyphus, pushes his old blue heart up to the
station.

While observing the conventional rhyme scheme, Diaz alters
the punctuation yet maintains the word order (another require-
ment of the form), thus changing the grammatical function
and meaning of the repeating lines. But these formal obser-
vances only highlight Diaz's innovations: the low-key free-verse
rhythms, the flat, plain language, the change of "blue Chevy"
to "blue heart" in the closing line, the poem's one gesture of
lyricism. This isn't merely an instance of a poet putting new
wine in old bottles: rather, it's an instance of a poet extending
a form, reshaping it, making it responsive to new and different
experience. The highly repetitive, overdetermined nature of
the triolet is adapted to the highly repetitive, overdetermined
nature of drug addiction. The new subject alters the handling
of the form, and the form itself alters our perception of the
subject. Like Jonson and Cunningham, Diaz is being personal
and traditional, conventional and original, immersed in literary history in order to express a distinctly contemporary and
individual point of view.

7

It's a truism to say we're by nature social animals, that we live
and thrive in relation to other people. What complicates this
picture, though, is the odd fact that social norms, conventions,
and mores not only mediate our interactions with each other

but also generate the terms by which we understand ourselves; they're like a metrical substrate by which the rhythms of our distinct identities are measured. If I think to myself, Good God I'm short, or way too loose with money, or a tightwad, a hothead or a bigmouth, or a wallflower, I'm defining myself in terms of norms of behavior I've internalized so deeply I've forgotten they don't originate inside me, even if inside me, usually late at night, just before sleep, is where I come to see myself as too much of a this or not enough of a that. The very language I think with connects me to a social world. The still small inner voice implies a listener, an other, even if the other is me, or that part of myself I've assimilated from the outer world, which may be how the world keeps watch on me when no one else is looking.

Paradoxically, one could say that if language is part and parcel of our self-awareness, a necessary if not sufficient condition of self-awareness, then awareness is both socially constituted and isolating, inherently social and private. Only I can feel and know what goes on inside me; only you can feel and know what goes on inside you. Not just physical sensation but also emotional and psychic states exist, initially at least, off stage, hidden away from public view, and unless I buckle over and collapse, or cry out in pain, what I experience I experience alone, with an immediacy no one else can really share. Which may be why, when it comes to other people's suffering, we are all doubting Thomases—unless we can stick our finger in the open wound we never quite believe in its reality; but when it comes to our own suffering, we're each of us nothing if not the crucified Son of God.

But here's another complication: If I say, "I hurt," the word *hurt* feels nothing. It's just a collection of arbitrary shapes connected to a collection of arbitrary sounds we organize into the word *hurt*. When I say "I hurt," the word looks up at me and

shrugs and goes back to being the nothing that it is until someone else it doesn't know or care about says "I hurt, too." All of
which is just to say that we express even our most private feelings by means of inert public signs. Our irreducibly personal
sense of ourselves depends for its articulation on a system of
signs that we did not invent, that exists independently of us and
is utterly indifferent to the mouths it momentarily inhabits,
the lives it momentarily expresses. A lion has more empathy
for the baby gazelle it devours than our precious words do for
those who speak them.

So we're left with a paradox: the inherently social/imper-
sonal medium of language conditions self-awareness, which in
turn produces that personal voice inside us that makes us feel
distinct from and other than the impersonal and public linguistic conventions we depend on to express that very private sense.

How, then, does self-expression happen? How by means of
convention do we convey a more than conventional experience?
If the artistic process exists on a continuum between extremes
of the absolute interiority of bodily sensation on the one hand
and of the mediating norms of language on the other, then
to use convention to express an unconventional feeling is to
effect a kind of reciprocal alchemy: a transmutation of private
incommunicable feeling into the public conventions of communication; and, conversely, of those public forms into the
particulars of subjectively intense experience. As in "My Picture Left in Scotland," "The Aged Lover," and Diaz's triolet, the
convention is personalized without ceasing to communicate,
and the personal is conventionalized without ceasing to convey
what's fresh and surprising, such that both are altered by their
integration into something social and keenly private, impersonal and new. Our desire to translate the irreducibly subjective into the social norms of expression without losing either

the integrity of feeling or the social world beyond the feeling, which the feeling depends on to be recognized, if not exactly shared, is what makes writing so necessary and difficult.

8

But what, then, do we do when experience is so extreme, so far beyond the pale of ordinary life, that it exceeds all means of expression? How without falsification or simplification do we give shape and meaning to the unspeakably horrible? Theodor Adorno famously wrote that poetry would be impossible after the Holocaust. And if by poetry he meant the conventionally beautiful or self-applauding shows of anguish at the suffering of others, he was probably right. But really bad things have been around as long as we have, even longer. If the Holocaust or any other devastations one could name, manmade and natural, have made artistic self-expression morally complicated, if not entirely obscene, it seems just as problematic, morally and otherwise, not to respond to such events with stories and poems, paintings and songs. As classics scholar Oliver Taplin has written, "The tragedies of real life, unlike those of the stage, are often shapeless, sordid, capricious, meaningless. But supposing this to be true (as I do), what then? It is not human to be content with this useless, even if ultimate, truth. We must try to understand, to cope, to respond. It is in this attempt that tragedy—that most great art—has its place."

Even extreme events that beggar the conventions of art must use those conventions even to say this much. That is, what a morally inclusive account of the Holocaust would entail is precisely an awareness built into the sound and structure of the inadequacy of the account it's giving. In the following poem by Dan Pagis, an Israeli Holocaust survivor who died in 1986, the sentence as a fundamental conveyer of meaning is invoked and exploded. One might even argue that the sentence becomes the grammatical symbol of the historical continuity that is the essence of Judaism, a religion and culture based primarily on collective memory that reaches back into the distant past and forward into the indefinite but emergent future. The norms of grammar that hold the sentence together embody the biblical traditions that hold the Jewish people together, traditions that the genocide of World War II very nearly destroyed, and did in fact destroy for those like Pagis who had experienced that catastrophe firsthand:

WRITTEN IN PENCIL IN THE SEALED RAILWAY-CAR

here in this carload
i am eve
with abel my son
if you see my other son
cain son of man
tell him that i

That the broken message is written in pencil (easily erased), on the wall of a boxcar where no one will read it, only intensifies our sense of rupture and erasure. Yet the fragment that remains derives its heartbreaking meaning from the very traditions and norms that have been obliterated; that is, the brokenness as brokenness can be conveyed only by means of the no-longer-existing whole. The poem depends on structures and expectations that aren't in any way original to Pagis. It's a dramatic monologue, for instance, a genre of literary art that has a long and distinguished history; it assumes we've read the Bible or at least know the book of Genesis. And of course it assumes we expect the sentence as sentence to complete itself, and that a speaker making a request will tell us what he or she wants us to do. It ironically assumes that the world in which requests are made and honored by being carried out still exists. By means of all these collective assumptions, conventions, traditions, Pagis makes a poem unlike any we've ever read.

9

I still love Ferlinghetti even if I regard him as a guilty pleasure. I'm indebted to the poems for having started me on the road to the life I've had the good fortune to live, a life of teaching and writing, and however limited his work may be, however dated, I acknowledge the transformative power it once possessed for me, even if the social program it proposed seems ludicrous now, some five decades later. Though it may be only of and for a particular moment, I understand and even honor the feeling it expressed, the need it spoke to.

As I get older, I grow more certain of the value of writing as I become less certain of what it is we're doing when we write. Back in the 1970s I possessed the deadly combination of confidence and ignorance. Now I feel a little like the speaker of Bob Dylan's great song "My Back Pages," the refrain of which is "But I was so much older then, I'm younger than that now." In the place of unassailable self-assurance about what makes poems and stories good, I now feel mostly a childlike amazement at the transformation that somehow happens in any kind of poem or story that's unforgettably distinct. How these inert signs can capture life so vitally is astonishing. While I know that convention permeates everything we think and do, everything we write, I don't know how the alchemy of self-expression happens, how the impersonal systems of communication blend with nuances of individual perception.

We're born into dense tangles of ongoing, ever-changing stories or plots that together form a heterogeneous mix of chemical, biological, cultural, and linguistic subplots; some of these subplots we share with all matter everywhere in the universe, some with everything that's ever lived on earth, some with just the members of our species, or our sex, or our country, or the region of the country we were born in, or just the people we live next door to, our friends and families. The stories comprising these elements are telling themselves through the stories we spend so much of our lives devising and refining in hope of leaving behind some trace of who we really are. They displace us even while they make us possible, even while we struggle to impose on them, or tease out from them, a record of ourselves that resonates with others while remaining distinctly if not uniquely ours.

10

In 1994 I'm living in North Carolina. My sister Beth has just been diagnosed with breast cancer. We don't know this at the time, but she has nineteen months to live. My brother is on the verge of divorcing his childhood sweetheart, the mother of his two young daughters. In 1997 he'll be diagnosed with brain cancer and be dead in about a year. I'm married for the second time, not happily, and we have two young children.

I've put together a new collection of poems, and the image I've chosen for the cover is the ancient photograph of my father's family that had pride of place on the wall of my childhood home. I study the people smiling out at me, all looking so much younger than I am now. My father's youngest sister is sitting next to her husband, who everyone would soon discover is an inveterate womanizer. Sometime in the next year or so he'll be away on business, when his wife will call his hotel room at 1:00 a.m. and a woman answers. And not long after that, she'll file for divorce. This is, in fact, the last family occasion he attends, the last picture he appears in.

Next to him is another brother-in-law looking to his left at his beautiful wife, who's looking out at us. He adores his wife, but he drinks too much. And she's just about had it. A few years earlier, after some vague business venture went belly up, he became a hairdresser, a profession associated with homosexuals ("faygelahs"). That he is good at cutting hair only increases his sense of having lost his manhood, having failed his family. His wife has threatened to leave him if he doesn't quit the boozing. He doesn't, but before she has the chance to leave him, he drops dead of a heart attack. This too is his last picture with the family.

Next to my father stands his eldest sister; she has two daughters, both of them mildly retarded.

I look at my jaunty father with his fedora pushed back on his head, his tie loosened, smiling so confidently, so cocksure of his good looks, of his classy wife, of his future great good fortune. Soon he will go to work for his brother Amos in the slaughterhouse, for peanuts ("bubkis"), and it will drive my mother crazy how he places loyalty to his brother over loyalty to her and their three young kids, a loyalty, she'll be quick to add, that his brother doesn't return. Amos will spend most of his time in Florida with his wealthy friends, playing golf, relaxing, while my father works like a dog, running the business seven days a week. And yet he'll never earn enough to pay for a pair of slippers, much less—God forbid—a trip somewhere. But eventually the two brothers will fall out over money, and for the last fifteen years of Amos's life they will not speak.

The war to end all wars is over. Everyone in the picture, at least for the moment of the picture, is dreaming the dreams given to their generation, dreams of glamour, wealth, the husbands tall, good-looking, and successful, the wives all beautiful and classy, the houses full of beautiful children who'll adore them, a life free of the struggles and anxieties that dogged their elders, that made their lives such a daily grind.

My parents will stay married for sixty-three years. They will fight constantly, they will threaten to break up yearly, monthly, and sometimes daily, but they never will. Every now and then they'll forget about their resentments and seem to take joy in each other's presence, but mostly they will sulk and brood in silence, and now and then explode.

So it almost seems like courage, the way they smile at the camera, the wholeheartedness with which they claim the moment as their own, the certainty that no bad thing can ever happen to them.

This is the image I've chosen for the cover of the book.

The title of the book is *Covenant*.

Mark Twain and the Creative Ambiguities of Expertise

The small seminar room was crowded with nearly forty other students as my instructor, J. V. Cunningham, read my poem aloud to the class. This was my freshman year at Brandeis University in 1970. I was eighteen, passionately in love with the open-style poetry of Kenneth Patchen, Lawrence Ferlinghetti, and Allen Ginsberg. For me poetry was a spiritual calling, an emotional free-for-all, and on the page at least a liberating rejection of the rank commercialism, status seeking, and sexual prudery of the middle-class world I came from. Cunningham was a chain-smoking lapsed Catholic, a sixty-something westerner with emphysema, a child of the Depression, a rigorous formalist, and a master of the epigram who did not suffer fools gladly and who assumed everyone was a fool until proven otherwise. For Cunningham all good poetry was first and foremost verse, and verse, as he says in *The Journal of John Cardan*,

is a professional activity, social and objective, and its methods and standards are those of craftsmanship. It is a concern of the ordinary human self, and is on the whole within a man's power to do well or not. Its virtues are the civic virtues. If it lacks much, what it does have is ascertainable and can be judged. But poetry [which is all I cared about back then] is amateurish, religious, and eminently unsociable. It dwells in the spiritual life, in the private haunts of theology or voodoo. . . . It is the accidental issue, the plain bastard, of grace and inspiration, or of the demons of anxiety—even of somatic irritation, for indigestion may be your angel.

Needless to say, ours was not a match made in heaven, unless heaven is run by Joseph Mengele, or so it seemed to me at the time.

Cunningham didn't teach creative writing the way it's taught today. You didn't make copies for everyone and didn't read the poem to the class. Instead, you gave Cunningham your copy and he read it out loud (without saying whose it was) and then asked the class to talk about it. As luck would have it, he chose my poem first. Barely above a whisper, he read the poem, pausing now and then to take a drag of his Lucky Strike. I'm sure everyone knew the poem belonged to me, the one student with his head under the desk, trying his shoelaces, contemplating some alternative career.

When he finished, he said to the class, "So what do you think?" After at least one-hundred-forty-seven years of silence, he held the poem up and said, "This is nothing more than spilled ink"; then he crumpled my masterpiece into a ball, threw it into the trashcan, and went on to the next poem, which I am happy to report fared no better.

Second day of class: The population shrank from forty to four. I was one of the four. A glutton for punishment, yes, I was. I admit it. But I was lucky because I had been a basketball player most of my life; I had even come to Brandeis to play basketball. Unlike my classmates, I was used to failing in public, I was used to being chewed out daily by my coaches. So while it hadn't been pleasant to have the poem I thought so highly of dismissed so rudely, I wasn't devastated. If anything, Cunningham had thrown down the gauntlet, and I was determined to prove to him that I could write. Every workshop he offered for the next two years I signed up for. Every literature class he taught (mostly Shakespeare and sixteenth-century poetry) I enrolled in. At the end of my sophomore year, we met and he told me that my work wasn't getting any better and that he didn't want to see anything of mine for a year. And if at the end of that year I showed improvement, he'd agree to continue working with me. So I dropped out of school.

After hitchhiking to San Francisco and running out of money, I hitchhiked to Lansing, Michigan, and lived in my sister's basement and wrote. And wrote. And wrote. When she threw me out, I returned to Boston and continued writing while I earned a living as a taxi driver till the fall semester began. I brought Cunningham the poems I'd written. He read through one or two of them, took a deep drag of his Lucky Strike, and said that when he told me I shouldn't show him work for a year he hadn't meant that I should drop out of school. The poems were just as bad now as they were then, he said, but that since I'd emotionally blackmailed him by going to the lengths I did, he agreed reluctantly to continue working with me.

While he came to have great affection for me (and I for him), Cunningham never much cared for anything I wrote. His comments, like his poems, were brief and nearly always dismissive: too much of the pretty-pretty here, or hardly seems worth the trouble, or meter falls flat on its face. He pronounced, he didn't explain. He didn't believe in spoon-feeding his students or giving too much of himself for fear of encouraging pedagogical dependency. Instead he simply pointed us in this or that direction, depending on our interests, so we could learn as actively and independently as possible. For all his dedication to verse as a social practice and dislike of spiritual mumbo-jumbo, he maintained that what makes a good poem good is hard to talk about and often better left unsaid. Reading a good poem was like having good sex: afterward all you wanted to do was smoke. During our last meeting at the end of my senior year, I showed him a new poem and he said, "Well, Mr. Shapiro, if I liked this sort of thing, I'd say you did it very well."

Thirty years later, I spent an interminable week as poet in residence in an MFA program out west. The senior poet of the program, let's call him Poet X, was a devout postmodern Christian who believed that language possesses its own mystical power, which the great writer channels by humbling himself before it, as if in prayer. On the page and in the classroom, he had integrated his predilection for defamiliarizing fragmentation with devotion to God. Irrational impulse and improvisation, even obscurity, in his view, bespoke spiritual humility, a disavowal of control and arrogance, a way for the poet/worshiper to break through the false coherence of the ego to the transcendently numinous. In Poet X's view, evil is closure and certainty; goodness is openness and indeterminacy. Closed forms reflect closed and dangerous minds, authoritarian minds, Hitlerian minds. Or as he put it, "The cost of form is the Holocaust." According to Poet X, the great twentieth-century example of poetic arrogance is Wallace Stevens; the great twentieth-century example of poetic humility is Ezra Pound. The more unwilled a poem is, the less insistent or dominant any one meaning will be, thus decentering the poet's authority and ego and thereby making room for God. Reading then becomes creatively participatory, an open-ended endeavor between reader and writer, and as such a model of social justice and spiritual love.

What's not to like?

As one would expect, his students were fellow travelers in the quasi-ecstatic quasi-academic poetics he promoted. The poetry they wrote aspired to articulate Derridean silences, negative linguistic spaces, the holy aporia within. I remember one poem I was asked to comment on, in which the lines were broken chaotically in the middle of words and staggered all over the page. When I suggested that the lineation might be a little bit confusing, the student said he wanted the reader to be confused. When I asked why he broke one particular line after the *b* in "ball," he explained that he wanted to break the word open so as to generate a play on the old army advertising slogan "Be all that you can be." Incomprehensible as the poem was, it wasn't for lack of intentionality. The poem was a veritable Guantánamo Bay of intention. I felt like I was being waterboarded with intentions: had the poem been any longer I'd've confessed to anything.

Don't get me wrong. I still very much believe that poetry in its highest state is an approach to the numinous. I still think of it as a kind of spiritual calling, though one not incompatible with verse as Cunningham describes it. I'm not against experimentation in the arts or opposed to mysticism on the page. The mansion of poetry has many rooms. While I have my preferences, I really don't have any programmatic ax to grind. And I like Pound, too, though *humility* isn't the first word that comes to mind when I think about his work. The contrast between Poet X's theory and his practice, between his touting of poetry as non-discursive openness to God and his deploying a self-conscious battery of reasons to explain and justify each and every microgesture on the page, is not unique to him or to the program he runs, or to the poetry he espouses. I think rather that Poet X embodies in extreme form an unavoidable and sometimes creative inconsistency at the heart of what we all do, both in the classroom and on the page.

Unless you're self-deceived or just dishonest, if you teach fiction or poetry of any kind you can't help but see it in some way, as Cunningham did, as a learnable skill, a social practice, with standards and conventions, established or emerging, that can be rationally discussed, agreed on, argued over, contested, and revised. Implicit in our programs of creative writing, in the very notion of creative writing as a course of study, is the acknowledgment that writing is a willed activity, something we choose to do and believe we'll do more successfully the more alert, more conscious, or more informed we are about what it is we're doing, which means becoming intimately conversant with the expressive traditions we both inherit and redefine. As writers and teachers of writing, we traffic in awareness. We all believe that through study and hard work we can refine our gifts. We sit in workshops and lecture halls in hope of becoming better writers and better readers, and in general more sensitive and self-aware linguistic animals. Whether we admit it or not, we all believe in the reality and value of expertise; we believe that there's nothing "natural" about the acquisition of expertise—that expertise or mastery (whatever we mean by that, and I'll say more about this later) doesn't grow organically inside us like a vegetable. Rather, it's something we diligently work at to achieve, something like a muscle that continuous exercise strengthens. This aspect of our practice presupposes and depends on or issues from qualities we don't normally think of as creative or imaginative: qualities like self-conscious disciplined cultivation of will, critical/rational intelligence, and breadth of knowledge. We believe with Cunningham that poetry can be taught.

But we also believe, and even Cunningham believed, with Poet X that you can only teach what you can talk about, and that perhaps the most essential aspect of a poem (its just-rightness, in Cunningham's vague term) cannot be talked about and thus cannot be taught.

Moreover, on and off the page, in and out of the classroom or lecture hall, when we describe our actual moment-by-moment engagement with the process of writing, our language tilts more to the amateurish, voodoo poetry side of the equation than to the verse side with all its civic virtues. We often speak in terms of necessity, not choice; of irrational inspiration, accident, or reverie, not rational calculation. We invoke the muse, or the unconscious or spiritus mundi, as a primary source of power. We say that writing is akin to spiritual revelation or mystical possession, or metempsychosis, that there is something magical or marvelous about the process, and that when it's really good it isn't really under our control, that it overcomes whatever we think our intentions are with intentions of its own, intentions we aren't aware of and would probably ruin if we were. We say that bad poems are bad partly because they don't draw energy from anything deeper than mere consciousness, or the merely conscious self. The buzzword for "too conscious" is *contrived*, and I bet every creative writing teacher, including me, has used it more than once in the last few months.

If I had a dollar for every time I quoted Robert Frost's remark that if there's no surprise for the writer there'll be no surprise for the reader, I might have voted Republican in the 2012 election. I can't tell you how many times in class I've heard myself disparage a passage in a poem for being rhetorical, in the Yeatsian sense of "will doing the work of imagination" (as if imagination were antithetical to will). How often in essays and lectures have you heard a poet or fiction writer extol the virtues of not knowing what he or she is doing as a way of getting closer to the wild or uncontrollable, or as a way of inducing mystical possession, or duende, as Federico García Lorca put it? (Imagine a writing program using the advertising pitch that it will teach you how not to know what you are doing better than any other program!)

On our scale of desired qualities or effects, we rank the intensely organic higher than the coolly mechanical; we prefer the risky, destabilizing strange or magical over the too-well-made, too orderly, too deliberately coherent. We give our uncritical assent to Archibald MacLeish, who tells us without irony that a poem should not mean but be even though in saying so he contradicts himself (a poem should not say "should not" and I just said so in my poem, so there). I think William Wordsworth is right to say that analytical intelligence does murder to dissect. And John Keats is right too to worry as he does in "Lamia" about how thinking can "clip an angel's wing, unweave the rainbow. . . . Do not all charms fly / at the mere touch of cold philosophy . . . ?" And yet Wordsworth also defines imagination as reason in its most exalted mood and bemoans the massive proliferation of stimuli in cities for having deadened and benumbed the faculties of discrimination and discernment. And Keats is nothing if not coldly, precisely analytical in some of the very poems that diagnose the dangers of intellectuality dissociated from emotion. When we talk about the writing process, we seem to harbor great ambivalence toward the knowledge and know-how we've dedicated so much of our writing life to acquiring, and so much of our teaching life to passing on.

There is a deep and inescapable duality at the heart of imaginative writing, a duality composed of what we normally think of as mutually exclusive qualities that in our best stories and poems are woven together so integrally that they become mutually entailing. The attention we pay to language and experience when we write well is like the attention we pay to poetry or stories when we read or teach well: it is both engaged and detached, critically analytical and sympathetic, passively inspired and actively aware, a function of both mind and heart in all their myriad forms. But (and this is where we get into trouble): to think or talk discursively about this more than discursive process is to tease out and separate and thus distort the many cognitive elements that constitute it. We fall into dichotomizing modes of thought that at our best as readers and writers aren't dichotomies at all but different facets of a single continuous act of attention. This conundrum is a little like the problem physicists face whenever they try to describe quantum mechanical realities in the language of classical physics: we can't conceive of matter except as either particle or wave, when at subatomic levels it behaves as neither one nor the other but as a profoundly weird amalgam of both—more like a wave in some experiments and more like a particle in others.

Recently I stumbled across a wonderful articulation of this problem or tension in Mark Twain's great book *Life on the Mississippi*, his memoir about his apprenticeship in the culture and science of steamboat piloting in the 1850s. In addition to a personal and cultural history, and a novel-like depiction of unforgettable, often hilarious characters, idioms, and stories, *Life on the Mississippi* is also a kind of parable about literary education, the ambiguities of expertise, how one gets from apprentice to master in the acquisition of a craft—poems and stories in our case, not steamboat piloting—and what one gains and loses in the process.

Twain explicitly compares the Mississippi River to a book, and steamboat piloting to a kind of reading. The process of learning how to read the river is slow and arduous, full of humbling screw-ups, and requiring phenomenal feats of memorization, for this book, in addition to being thousands of miles

long, is "the crookedest river in the world since in one part
of its journey it uses up one thousand three hundred miles to
cover the same ground that the crow would fly over in six hundred and seventy five." As if that's not hard enough, the shape
of the river is always changing, "making prodigious jumps by
cutting through narrow necks of land and thus straightening
and shortening itself," or "changing its habitat bodily by moving sidewise," so much so that, for instance, the town of Delta,
Twain says, "used to be three miles below Vicksburg," but "a
recent cut off has radically changed its position, and Delta is
now two miles above Vicksburg." Not only that, but the river's
snags are always hunting up new quarters, its sandbars are
never at rest, its channels forever dodging and shirking, and all
this must be confronted in all nights and all weathers without
the aid of a single lighthouse or buoy. So if the river is a book,
it's a book the skillful steamboat pilot is always reading for the
first time in a language he is also just beginning to learn. Or as
Twain puts it, "Two things seemed pretty apparent to me. One
was, that in order to be a pilot a man had got to learn more than
any one man ought to be allowed to know, and the other was that
he must learn it all over again in a different way every twenty
four hours."

Twain's struggle to master steamboat piloting resonates with
frustrations all of us have felt at every phase of our apprenticeship to poetry and fiction. In my view, the Mississippi (at least
as Twain describes it) doesn't resemble a book so much as a
language or a literary tradition that, like the river, isn't fixed
or static but is forever emerging and disappearing, dynami-
cally changing and being changed by the nationalities, civili-
zations, and material cultures flowing through it, or making up
its current—all of which the aspiring writer has to assimilate
as best he can in order to master the craft. From this perspec-

tive, you can read *Life on the Mississippi* as a meditation on the nature of tradition and what can and can't be learned, and what exactly we mean when we talk about expertise in relation to the impossible task of mastering something so vast and inherently and vitally unstable, such that the best you can hope for is to know only enough about it to know you'll never know enough.

Twain's education, fraught as it is with humiliating failures, is not without self-deprecating humor. Like all of us starting out, he begins his journey down the Mississippi with the easy confidence of late adolescence. He assumes that "all a pilot had to do was to keep his boat in the river," and how hard could that be "since it was so wide"? His two-year apprenticeship to Horace Bixby, his mentor-tormentor, swings manically between moments of inflated self-confidence based on ignorance and complacency, and self-deflating realizations of inadequacy. Whenever Twain thinks he knows more than he does, Bixby reminds him of, crushes him with really, all he hasn't yet begun to learn, and how impossible yet necessary it is to get the entire river down by heart, to memorize everything from how to tell a bluff reef from a wind reef, or how much water they had in the middle crossing at Hole in the Wall during the trip before last, to the exact marks the boat lay in when they had the most shoalful water, in every one of the five hundred shoal places between St. Louis and New Orleans, and how he mustn't get the shoal soundings and marks of one trip mixed up with the shoal soundings and marks of another, for no two are alike. Usually these lessons end with Twain saying in complete despair, "When I get so that I can do all that, I'll be able to raise the dead."

Apart from the enviably deluded among us, who hasn't felt utterly defeated by the sheer volume of great literature we're required to learn, much less to emulate? Who hasn't undergone similar manic swings of elation and deflation when we started writing and everything was new, when on good days we wrote about "the splendor in the grass" for the sheer intrinsic joy of writing, and on bad days we realized we weren't communing with the muse at all but simply sitting in a room talking to ourselves? Who among us hasn't at some point felt so intimidated by what we didn't know that we made a virtue out of knowing nothing and fell back on such hackneyed romantic/postromantic notions as the sacrosanct individual voice that must be quarantined from the contaminating influence of any other voice?

The saddest and most interesting moment in Twain's account of his education on the Mississippi comes unexpectedly, not during the training itself but after it's been completed, when the book of the river has opened its secrets to him as clearly as if it uttered them with a voice. "There was never so wonderful a book written by man," he says, "never one whose interest was so absorbing, so unflagging, so sparkingly renewed with every re-perusal." The passenger who couldn't read this book saw the river as merely a kind of canvas—a pretty surface painted by sun and clouds, a sensory experience to be enjoyed. But for the trained eye of the pilot, the river was "the grimmest and most dead earnest of reading matter."

In the long passage below, the triumph we've been led to expect comes at a cost. The apparent good–bad opposition between trained and untrained vision, between the professional eye that's learned to read the deeper meaning of what lies before it and the naive eye delighting in mere appearances, turns out to be neither simply good nor simply bad. The sense of triumph in what follows is hard to distinguish from a sense of loss:

Now when I had mastered the language of this water and had come to know every trifling feature that bordered the great river as familiarly as I knew the letters of the alphabet, I had made a valuable acquisition. But I had lost something too. I had lost something, which could never be restored to me while I lived. All the grace, the beauty, the poetry had gone out of the majestic river. I still keep in mind a certain wonderful sunset, which I witnessed when steam boating was new to me. A broad expanse of the river was turned to blood; in the middle distance the red hue brightened into gold, through which a solitary log came floating, black and conspicuous; in one place a long, slanting mark lay sparkling upon the water; in another the surface was broken by boiling, tumbling rings, that were as many-tinted as an opal; where the ruddy flush was faintest, was a smooth spot that was covered with graceful circles and radiating lines, ever so delicately traced; the shore on our left was densely wooded, and the somber shadow that fell from this forest was broken in one place by a long, ruffled trail that shone like silver; and high above the forest wall a clean-stemmed dead tree waved a single leafy bough that glowed like a flame in the unobstructed splendor that was flowing from the sun . . . and over the whole scene, far and near, the dissolving lights drifted steadily, enriching it, every passing moment, with new marvels of coloring. . . . The world was new to me and I had never seen anything like this at home. . . . But a day came when I began to cease from noting the glories and the charms which the moon and the sun and the twilight wrought upon the river's face; another day came when I ceased altogether to note them. Then, if that sunset scene had been repeated, I should have looked upon it without rapture, and should have commented upon it inwardly after this fashion: this sun means that we are going to have wind tomorrow; that flowing log means that the river is rising; that slanting mark on the water refers to a bluff reef which is going to kill somebody's steamboat one of these nights, if it keeps on stretching out like that; those tumbling boils show a dissolving bar and a changing channel there; the lines and circles in the slick water over yonder are a warning that that troublesome place is shoaling up dangerously . . . that tall dead tree, with a single living branch is not going to last long, and then how is a body ever going to get through this bland place at night without the friendly old landmark.

No, the romance and the beauty were all gone from the river. All the value any feature of it had for me now was the amount of usefulness it could furnish toward compassing the safe piloting of a steamboat. Since those days, I have pitied doctors from my heart. What does the lovely flush in a beauty's cheek mean to a doctor but a "break" that ripples above some deadly disease. Are not all her visible charms sown thick with what are to him the signs and symbols of hidden decay? Does he ever see her beauty at all, or doesn't he simply view her professionally, and comment upon her unwholesome condition all to himself? And doesn't he sometimes wonder whether he has gained most or lost most by learning his trade?

Twain presents us with two versions of the same scene—the first is the sunset perceived by the untrained eye of a passenger, an eye with no purpose other than to see for the sake of seeing; what it loses in meaning it makes up for in excitement and beauty; the second scene is perceived by the trained eye of the expert, the eye that sees professionally, the specialist's eye, the eye responsible for the boat's safe passage through dangerous waters.

The language of the first sunset is painterly—imagistic, sensory, highly figurative; the language of the second is chastened—analytical and abstract. The passivity of received impression in the first scene is reflected in the proliferation of weak verbs, on the one hand, and rich figurative imagery, on the other: "was" or "were" is repeated at least ten times, while flowery elevated adjectives modify the vast majority of nouns. Even the "clean-stemmed" dead tree above the forest wall is described as "waving a single leafy bough and glowing like a flame in the unobstructed splendor that was flowing from the sun."

The second sunset, by contrast, is stylistically more active and restrained. The verbs are stronger but more abstract, even while Twain strips the scene of adjectival elaboration—the verbs emphasize perception not for its own sake but for the sake of safe navigation. They evoke not objects but relationships among objects: this sun *means* that there'll be wind tomorrow, that floating log *means* the river will be rising, that slanting mark on the water *refers* to a bluff reef, those tumbling boils *show* a dissolving bar. The "clean-stemmed" dead tree waving its leafy bough of the first scene becomes in the second a "tall dead tree with a single living branch" that will fall soon, and then the "bland place" will be harder to get through without that landmark to navigate by. Where the untrained innocent eye sees a literary "bough," the experienced eye sees the realistic branch. The difference between the two sunsets is not unlike the difference that Wordsworth describes in "Intimations of Immortality," between the young poet/child of nature, for whom the world appears appareled in "the glory and freshness of a dream," and the mature poet with his less intense but richer, deeper, more sober understanding that makes up in knowledge what it loses in animal intensity.

By the end of the passage, I feel as if I've been presented with two complementary, not antithetical, pictures. There is great beauty in the first sunset. So much so, I can't help but think Twain cheats a little here in that the passenger / cub pilot / young writer he describes might not be an expert in steamboat piloting but he sure as hell is an expert in writing, in describing a scene vividly and freshly. And it isn't that the first sunset is more vivid than the second—they're both vivid but in different ways, engaging different faculties. The description of the first sunset draws almost exclusively on the sensory imagination, on the physical texture of the here and now looked at for its own sake, not for the sake of any meaning, whereas the language of the second is more intellectual or analytical, more concerned with cause and effect, with making inferences from what's before it about what one may encounter tomorrow or sometime after that. The first eye deprived of the second is a little too precious; but the second deprived of the first is just as incomplete, more of a blueprint of a sunset on the river than the thing itself.

The doctor analogy captures poignantly Twain's sense of loss in the acquisition of skill, in the cultivation of a way of looking that suppresses beauty or appreciation in the name of some other aim. He shows us the price of a single-minded hyper-specialized habit of mind. Mastery like this, however necessary, is incomplete—taken to extremes, it can lead to the logical insanity of statements like "the operation was a success but the patient died" and "we had to destroy the village in order to save it." Haven't we all been guilty of this from time to time, catching ourselves taking too specialized a stance toward our own and other people's lives, becoming (God forbid) professionals of experience, artistic ambulance chasers, thinking in the midst of some hardship, our own or someone else's, how we might go about writing it up? Or worse: maybe responding strictly in terms of craft and structure to a friend's or a student's heartfelt poem?

Many years ago at Northwestern University, I had a student who embodied the worst of all these tendencies. He was not untalented but a pure product of the pre-professional culture of higher education: he was less interested in learning than in doing what he had to do to graduate with honors so he could go to graduate school and become, what else, a lawyer. His poems were highly intellectual, all head and no heart, utterly divorced from his emotional life, so much so that when I suggested that his poems could use a blood transfusion he thought I was speaking literally, and next class he turned in a poem called "Blood Transfusion." Finally, he wrote a poem about someone (not him, of course) who lived only from the shoulders up, someone utterly cut off from himself and from other people. I got really excited. I thought at last the kid was getting it. When he came to see me, I told him how happy I was to see this poem, that in confronting his isolation and detachment, his inability to feel or connect with others, he had made a real breakthrough. "So," he said, "what you're saying is if I can write a few more poems like this one I'll get an A?"

An ideal doctor, of course, would be capable of both appreciating beauty and analyzing symptoms, of empathic care and professional distance—in the same way that a writer or teacher ideally exercises both sympathetic imagination and intellectual clarity in response to her own or other people's work. The good artist, like the good doctor, cultivates sensitivity and critical thought, even though under the pressure of circumstance his attention at times may tend more to the one or the other. The fact is there are no hard and fixed boundaries around faculties of mind. Our various capacities for thought and feeling may be different, but they are not distinct.

Horace Bixby time and again tells the young Twain that to learn his trade he has to learn the river by heart. *Learn by heart*—surely one of the most beautiful expressions in the English language. It's more than a metaphor for memory; rather it's a profound insight into what happens inside us when we read or write well: we feel the implication of thoughts; we think through the implications of feelings. Each becomes an extension of the other, and both engage as if for the first time the ever-shifting landscapes of language and life. The two sunsets taken together give us a model of a full response, a response that lives intensely throughout a wide range of faculties. The two together also give, by implication, a more compelling and persuasive definition of what we mean by *expertise*—a definition that lies closer to the word's Latin root, *experiri*, which means to try or test. An expert puts knowledge to the test of experience. Mastery is not a fixed state you arrive at or achieve once and for all; it isn't methodical or algorithmic; it can't be put on automatic pilot. A method-driven form of expertise, whether of the postmodern or new formalist variety, however much it gestures toward the irrational or the numinous or the surreal, is a defense against experience, a form of control masquerading as impulse or improvisation. That kind of mastery we're right to guard against. The kind of expertise that *Life on the Mississippi* embodies is a state of perpetual testing, of perpetual readiness; its triumphs and discoveries are at best a matter of moments, because the landscape of language, art, and life is never fixed. What you learn today you may need to unlearn tomorrow, or relearn in a different way so as to keep what you've learned responsive and flexible, ever alert to the widest range of possibility. Whether you write in traditional or experimental measures, it's the expert in you that sharpens memory, builds on what you've learned by heart, and keeps all your mental faculties supple and keen. It's never the form that makes a poem good or bad, conventional or not; it's how you handle the form, what you do with it, how you test it at every stage of composition. It's the expertise in you that keeps what you discover today from becoming a deadening mannerism tomorrow, that enables you to make each engagement with the page a fresh encounter, a more inclusive reckoning.

Needless to say, this isn't easy to do, early or late in one's career. From time to time we all feel as if we've lost some degree of crispness and excitement as we make the slow transition from the deluded confidence of our early work to a more mature sense of what it is we're doing, a maturity that's often indistinguishable from a disillusioned grasp of our own irrelevance. The trick (and it's one we're never finished learning) is, as Pound reminds us, to make it new, which doesn't mean forgetting what we've learned or dispensing with everything ever written before last Tuesday. It means rather to stay alert and active, to exercise both the taut passivity of a receptive mind and the active engagement of a mind adding to its store of knowledge, surpassing what it's learned, venturing out into the unknown where anything can happen. We are experts only insofar as our training gets us ready for that.

Replace "doctor" with "writer" in the following passage from *Atonement*, by Ian McEwan, and you find a perfect statement of what we talk about when we talk about expertise:

> For this was the point, surely: he would be a better doctor
> for having read literature. What deep readings his modi-
> fied sensibility might make of human suffering, of the self-
> destructive folly or sheer bad luck that drive men toward
> ill health! Birth, death, and frailty in between. Rise and
> fall—this was the doctor's business, and it was literature's

too. He was thinking of the nineteenth century novel. Broad tolerance and the long view, an inconspicuously warm heart and cool judgment; his kind of doctor would be alive to the monstrous patterns of fate, and to the vain and comic denial of the inevitable; he would press the enfeebled pulse, hear the expiring breath, feel the fevered hand begin to cool and reflect, in the manner that only literature and religion teach, on the puniness and nobility of mankind.

The doctor with literary training engages warm heart and cool judgment, sense and intellect; she draws on empathy and critical awareness, the long metaphysical view and the up-close and personal perspective. In the good doctor's or the good writer's practice, there are elements of both the civic virtues of verse and the inchoate longings of poetry, of what can be consciously acquired and what can only come through the unwilled grace of inspiration. Cunningham and Poet X are aiming at the same target from opposite positions. As good students, which even the best teachers have to be, we have to learn from both without limiting ourselves to either.

And this brings me to my last concern, and that is, the potential dangers of excessive training. One may need to know everything, but one also needs to know that knowing everything isn't everything. As the saying goes: the problem with the Know-It-All is that he doesn't know anything else. Twain returns to the Mississippi River twenty-five years later to revisit the scenes of his youth in the heyday of steamboating. And what disturbs him isn't merely the decline of steamboat culture. He is also shocked by the improvements that the government has made to the river itself, improvements which have dramatically increased the safety of navigation but, in doing so, have taken the skill and romance out of the profession:

The national government has turned the Mississippi into a sort of two-thousand-mile torchlight procession. In the head of every crossing, and in the foot of every crossing, the government has set up a clear-burning lamp. You are never entirely in the dark, now; there is always a beacon in sight, either before you, or behind you, or abreast. One might almost say that lamps have been squandered there. Dozens of crossings are lighted which were not shoal when they were created, and have never been shoal since; crossings so plain, too, and also so straight, that a steamboat can take herself through them without any help, after she has been through once. Lamps in such places are of course not wasted; it is much more convenient and comfortable for a pilot to hold to them than on a spread of formless blackness that won't stay still [a formless blackness Twain describes earlier as an atmosphere of black cats]. . . . But this thing has knocked the romance out of piloting.

Twain goes on to mention a few other government improvements that have destroyed the romance of the profession: how snag boats have removed "all the river's teeth," rooting out dangerous clusters of dead and fallen trees a boat might founder on, and how electric lights have made it easy to maneuver through narrow chutes at night, and how more sophisticated charts and compasses have made it possible to run through fog with security and confidence unknown in the old days. He was too wise and experienced a pilot not to recognize the blessings of these changes. At the same time, he concedes mournfully that these changes have taken away all the romance of the calling, have taken away "its state and dignity." It's in our American DNA to methodize the teaching if not the practices of art, to reduce it to a knack or know-how that anyone can learn. And that's fine, so long as the megabusinesses of our how-to books and graduate programs build into themselves a realistic and honest sense of what their limits are, of what they can and cannot do. Art, I believe, is transcendent and social, organic and mechanical. Like a centaur, what makes it magical is not irrational energy or rational control but the mix of both. Our programs, like our art, will suffer if they pretend to be all horse or human, all romance or impartible technique. Art is hybrid, in and out of the classroom, on and off the page.

My Tears See More
Than My Eyes

We parents signed in and entered the waiting area of the boys' ward that doubled as a family room during visiting hours. We migrated to the far corners of the room, as far away as possible from one another, as if afraid of contagion. Maybe it was easier that way for us to think, "My kid is different from theirs; he isn't really fucked up or suicidal, or violent; he's just going through a rough patch, a phase." We sat in silence, waiting for our sons; under bright fluorescent lighting that gave us all a sickly pallor, we looked anywhere but at each other; we looked at the rubber furniture, the grimly cheerful yellow walls, the message boards here and there scribbled over with institutional graffiti: goals for the day, prayers, bromides, warnings, rules. We were seeking some measure of privacy in a room in which no privacy was allowed.

Then the kids straggled in. They seemed dazed, as if wakened too abruptly from a deep sleep. Nat waved and smiled weakly. As he approached, I thought I saw my father's face in his, which surprised me as Nat and my dad share hardly any features. After we embraced and he sat down, I realized it wasn't any physical resemblance that brought my dad to mind, but Nat's depressive demeanor: the slump of his posture, the shuffling gait, the lack of affect in his eyes, the defeated, nearly vacant stare. He seemed like an old man, not a fifteen-year-old boy.

I noticed he was holding a black journal, cradling it in both hands like a hymnal. This was my first visit, the first time I'd been allowed to visit since he was transferred here two days earlier. He'd been on suicide watch, which meant no visitors and no leaving the ward. He couldn't go down to the gym for exercise or to the cafeteria for meals. At all times he was under someone's eye, even when he slept in the doorless room new patients had to use. This was his second hospitalization in the span of six weeks.

He wanted to know when he could come home. He assured me he'd learned his lesson, he'd never try to harm himself again. "I'm not crazy," he said, "I'm just sad, and this place is making me sadder. It's making me crazy, Dad. You gotta take me home."

As he spoke, I thought about the last few months. Nat had been out of school since early December, when an unrequited love with an older girl, a senior at his school, triggered an obsessive downward spiral that included binge drinking, blackouts, and late-night delirious messages left on the girl's answering machine. He was hospitalized in January when he became temporarily psychotic from the medication he was put on, and then again in February after a genuine suicide attempt. I thought about the weird, terribly isolated life he'd fallen into—apart from biweekly visits to his therapist and two hours each morning at the Hill Center, a remedial program for LD kids, he was alone all day with Callie and me. I could rarely get him out of his room. I'd stand at his door and call out his name, shouting to be heard over the rap or hip-hop on his stereo. Usually he wouldn't reply. Then I'd enter without being asked, afraid he might have hurt himself, and he'd explode. I was anxious about leaving him alone and equally anxious about intruding.

From time to time his mood would briefly lift, and we would play pool or work in the garden, or go to the Y and shoot baskets. But mostly he spent his days holed up in his room, the music blasting out a barrier of sound.

One morning as we were driving home from the Hill Center, I asked him what he wanted to do today. "How about we go straight to the gym?"

"No, Dad," he said, "I just want to go home, I have a lot on my plate."

"What do you mean you have a lot on your plate? What do you have to do?"

"Well, I have to do my Hill Center homework."

"That will take, what, ten minutes? Maybe half an hour?"

"Well," he said, smiling one of his rare smiles, "it's a small plate."

In the evenings, when his sister Izzy and stepbrother Aaron came home from school, he would rally for a little while and pretend to be OK, but eventually he'd return to his room, the door closed, the music cranked up high so none of us could hear him weeping. I thought about his inaccessibility and the anxiety that all of us felt at all times, Izzy and Aaron especially.

I thought about the two nights I found him dead drunk in his room, ranting about the girl and how if he wasn't such a loser she would love him, and how this was God's way of telling him he didn't deserve to live. I thought about those long nights sitting up with him till dawn, till he finally slept, and how when he woke a few hours later he remembered nothing of the night before, and anyway didn't give a shit whether he lived or died.

I thought about the first time we had to hospitalize him. Early that evening he seemed just fine, playing pool with Aaron. Then sometime after dinner, Aaron came into the kitchen while Callie and I were cleaning up and said, do you hear that? Nat was downstairs in a manic rage, trashing his room. He'd hurled everything on his desk—pens, papers, notebooks, laptop, printer—all over the room and knocked over all the furniture. By the time we got there, he was beating the wall with a standing lamp, paint chips and plaster scattered everywhere. He stopped when we told him to stop, but then he began to hallucinate. He was staring at Callie, saying her nose had fallen off and her face was bleeding. He said he had to get out of there and tried to run away. I held him down while Callie rushed upstairs to call the police. Nat broke free and bolted into the woods behind the house. I stumbled after him, afraid I'd never see him again. I had never been so terrified. The police found him some forty minutes later. Nat was insanely furious when they brought him home, not wanting to be touched, telling me to get the hell away. Later in the ER waiting room, when his manic anger suddenly lifted, he was like a little boy again, head resting on my shoulder, asking me if he was crazy, his voice utterly demoralized.

Most of all, I thought about my inability to keep him safe, and my overwhelming sense of having failed him, which mirrored his overwhelming sense of having failed himself as well as me and everybody else who loved him. I'd become so disheartened in recent weeks that I took to picturing Nat inside a coffin, as if to ready myself for what I couldn't keep from happening.

We should have realized that Nat had been depressed for years. I mean, we knew he wasn't as happy as most kids were, but we thought his depressive tendencies were intensified, if not produced, by his learning disabilities, which had made school such a trial for him. Now we realize that we had it backward, that his academic struggles were a function of a chronically depressed state of mind. He's a sweet, empathic, deeply intuitive child. An old soul is how I would describe him. Years ago, his first-grade teacher tried to soften the news about how poorly Nat was doing academically by saying, "But he does possess a real genius for friendship." And that is true. He has always been a charmer, someone older and younger kids alike are drawn to and admire, not so much for anything he does as for his emotional openness and sensitivity.

But these admirable empathic qualities in turn have made him overly concerned for others, too much at the mercy of how other people feel. Emotional intelligence and imagination, so central to moral decency, if taken to an extreme, can lead to a disabling vulnerability, a sense of self too unfixed or fluid for the kind of stability daily life requires. As George Eliot says in *Middlemarch*, "If we had a keen vision and feeling of all ordinary human life, it would be like hearing the grass grow and the squirrel's heart beat, and we should die of that roar which lies on the other side of silence. As it is, the quickest of us walk about well wadded with stupidity."

Nat has never walked about well wadded with stupidity. He's never achieved the animal insensitivity that often passes for a healthy sense of self. He's always been too much at the mercy of everybody else's psychic weather. And so despite his genius for friendship, or maybe because of it, as he got older and his circle of friends widened, it became more and more exhausting for him to bring together friends who didn't know each other for fear they might not get along. Among other things, this has made his birthday parties over the years more of an ordeal for him than a pleasure.

And then of course there were the devastating family losses. While he didn't really know my sister, he saw and still remembers keenly the toll her dying took on me and on our family. Three years later, Nat watched my brother decline and his parents' marriage fall apart. Three years after that, I collapsed while playing basketball on Nat's thirteenth birthday. Callie, he, and I celebrated in the hospital where two days later I'd have surgery to implant a pacemaker. Only fifteen, he's already had a lifetime's share of death and sorrow. Clinical depression may be caused in part by nature, not nurture, genetic bad luck, hard-wiring, or chemical imbalances in the brain, but what Nat has also had to live through has deeply shaped and even justified the blackest of his moods.

"So can I come home?" he asked again.

I told him at this point it wasn't our decision to make. There was nothing we could do but get through the next week or so, until we could figure out what the next best step for him would be.

"But you're my dad. Can't you get me out of here?"

I didn't know what to say, so I gestured toward the black journal in his hands. "Nat, have you been writing?"

"Sort of," he said. "I'm mostly freestyling, making it up in my head, and sometimes I write it down."

He leaned closer to me and whispered, "Dad, I snuck a pencil into my room, I've got it hidden under my mattress, and I write lines down at night when no one's watching."

From time to time over the years, Nat would write poems—they were always interesting and sometimes very beautiful. When he was really little, he used to say that when he grew up he wanted to become a poet like his dad. But as he got older and found reading and writing such a frustrating and joyless chore, his literary aspirations waned. I don't know how old he was, maybe six or seven, when he came into my book-lined study, looked around, and said despairingly, "Dad, if I want to become a poet, do I have to read all these books?"

In times of crisis, though, he turned to writing without any prompting from me. In 1998, while my brother was dying, Nat, nine years old at the time, wrote this:

THE WINTER AIR
For my Uncle Dave

The Flowers bloom.
The shadow of death is in the snowy air.
The flowers die away.
I feel scared and alone.
I want to be in bed.
A blue deer runs across the forest with leaping strides.

Around this time, it may have been a year or so earlier, Nat and his fellow classmates had to write and present a story to the school. The title of the stories the other students wrote were just what you'd expect: "Cary's Cat," "My Trip to the Zoo," "Why I Love My Teddy Bear." Nat's story was called "The Problem." As I said, the boy has an old soul. As a father, I found his precocious sensitivity to death and loss disturbing, almost unnatural, as if he grew up too fast, as if the accidents of fortune had robbed him of his childhood. Nine-year-old boys aren't meant to be haunted by the "shadow of death . . . in the snowy air." At the same, how could I not admire the poem, especially the wonderful blue deer leaping across the last line?

I read "The Winter Air" to Robert Pinsky. He was poet laureate at the time. Robert liked the poem too, and joked that it would be unethical of me as Nat's father to steal from it, but as a family friend he'd have no trouble doing so. One night, a few days later, Nat couldn't get to sleep. In those last hard months of my marriage to his mother, with the household rife with sorrow and mostly but not always unexpressed resentments, he often had trouble sleeping. On this night, though, he was running himself down for being stupid at school, for not being tall enough, or good enough at basketball, and so I told him that I shared his poem for Uncle Dave with Robert Pinsky, the poet laureate, and that Robert said the poem was terrific. Nat sat up, hugged himself, and sighed, "The most famous poet in America thinks I wrote a good poem!" He fell back on his pillow and went right to sleep.

"Would you show me something you've been writing?" I asked him.

His eyes widened with an excitement I hadn't seen in months.

He said, "Tell me what you think of this, I'm still working on it, but what do you think?" Then without opening the journal he recited this:

My insane brain can't contain
This hospital. This is the capital
Of hell, a spell
To compel me
To do nothing well.

My response to the poem, of course, was complicated. It broke my heart to hear Nat express such misery and despair, such anger. Yet the tone isn't merely despairing or angry, or if it is it also takes incredible pleasure in the anger, and gives pleasure in the expressing of it. I was, I don't know, elated, exhilarated, and profoundly encouraged by the eloquence and tonal energy of the verse, the lively almost sixteenth-century rhyming, and the powerful control, embodied by those proliferating rhymes over powerful feeling. The poem is athletic in its formal poise, even hopeful and affirmative, even while the subject matter refuses hope or affirmation.

The poem made me hopeful. For the first time in a long time, I could see Nat actively resisting the very despair he was articulating, a despair that off the page, outside the poem, seemed to have complete control of him.

"Nat, that's a wonderful poem," I said. "I mean it, it's really wonderful."

"It's just something I made up," he said, shaking his head sadly, as if to suggest that because he made it up, because he was the one who wrote it, it couldn't be any good.

"Let me hear another one."

He flipped through the pages of his journal. He read a couple of lyrics in the style and idiom of a black rapper, his chameleon imagination assuming the identity of his favorite artists. These were poems mostly about the other kids in the hospital, the vast majority of whom were African American, as well as a couple about the staff, in particular Mr. Stanley, a black counselor Nat came to love. There were rhymes I loved and memorable phrases ("the sound of rage make you live in a cage"; "But now the feeling feels like forever, the weather ain't never gonna change"), but overall the poems seemed like exercises, or unassimilated borrowings, too conventional in language and detail, even down to the "niggas," "glocks," and "AK-47s." At the same time, I could see and appreciate the psychological and artistic work they were accomplishing. Young poets learn by imitating, and they imitate the work they know. And rap music is the beat poetry of Nat's generation, though it's more popular in the general culture than beat poetry ever was. In Nat's case, in his homage to rap, he appropriates the rage and violence that is so much the staple of rap music (and in the best of it both reflects and protests against the violent world of the ghetto); he turns that rage against the hospital, against his own depression, against the older girl who failed to return his love. In these poems, he gets to be the bad boy he for various reasons never got to be at home. He gets to strike back at the very depression that he was otherwise passively suffering. Rap gave a powerless boy a feeling of power. It also gave him a feeling of community—a community of outcasts and victims—in the midst of extreme isolation.

Then he read me this epigrammatic poem about the girl:

I no longer
Want you
To be my hunger;
I need somebody
Younger.

J. V. Cunningham, my old teacher, and one of the great epi-grammatists of the twentieth century, would have loved this. Ben Jonson would have loved this. It's tight, efficient, lean; with a dancer's agility, the sentence leaps gracefully from line to line, and the phrasing is both startling and plain, which is an ideal of the classical plain style that Jonson and Cunningham perfected. The comedic timing of that witty last word "Younger" is, in my humble, unbiased opinion, completely pleasing.

"Nat," I said, "I mean it, this stuff is just so . . ."

"Listen, Dad," he interrupted, "I know it's your birthday tomorrow, and, well, I want you to have this." He handed me the journal.

"Nat, this is an incredible gift, it's the best gift anyone's ever given me, but you could give this to me when you get out. Don't you want to keep the journal with you so you can keep on writing?"

"No," he said, "I can still freestyle in my head, and I'll remember what I come up with, if it's any good. Anyway, I'm mostly writing things down at night in my room when I'm not supposed to, and I'm worried about them finding the pencil."

Mr. Stanley came into the common room to let us know visiting time was over.

"Okay, Nat," I said, "I'll take it, it's something I'll cherish, but if you need it back, you'll tell me, right?"

He said he would. We embraced, and I told him I'd see him on Saturday. "Promise?" he asked, so much like a little boy.

"Promise," I said.

When I got home, I read straight through the journal. I could tell from the handwriting—so wild and jagged with the ghosts of erased lines hovering behind and between the lines he kept— that Nat had done most of the writing at night, in secret, with his contraband pencil. On some pages there were fragments of phrases, new words he'd learned that day from the black kids on the ward ("New word DOLLARS = friends"), transcriptions of dreams, poems Xed out, under which in one case he scrawls: "I don't wanna continue—this rhyme sucks anyways." In his conversations with me, Nat had denied having any problems severe enough to justify hospitalization; in the poems, though, he speaks directly and unflinchingly about his misery and his wanting not to live. He wouldn't allow himself to bullshit on the page. For him, poetry was and is the place of truth-telling.

The most stunning expression of his despair came in one of the later poems. Underneath it he wrote a note addressed to me, instructing me on how to read the poem. The note read: "dad when you read this one you have to read the rhyming parts like you're in a panic, and then read the last line as if your son died right then and there."

Body's weakening,
Heart's beating
Too fast
For it to last.
I feel a blast
Of death
Running through my breath . . .
My tears see more than my eyes . . .

The "blast of death" could have come from Herbert's "Church Monuments" ("The blast of death's incessant motion / Fed with the exhalation of our crimes . . ."), though I'm pretty sure Nat has no idea who George Herbert is.

Reading it over now, I wonder if my desire to appreciate this poem as a poem isn't partly a defense against Nat's pain and helplessness. It's easier, after all, to analyze its formal poise than to imagine my own son feeling such emotional desperation. At the same time, I do believe that that control, that shaping— the way, for instance, the opening stanza strikes an impressive balance, with two rhyming couplets framing or holding in place the panicky triple rhyme of *fast-last-blast*—does represent a kind of victory over pain, however momentary; at the very least, it enables me to think some part of his imagination is holding together what he otherwise experiences as falling apart.

As I sat in my study staring at the poem, stunned by its beauty and heartbreak and the suddenly widening of attention from self to other, from son to father, an empathic leap of imagination rare for anyone at any age to make, but especially so for an adolescent boy, I remembered the night that Nat was born, the first time I held him. I remembered looking down at him and thinking, this is the most beautiful baby I have ever seen. Then I thought, maybe I think this because I am his father. So I took a step back and looked at him objectively, as if he wasn't mine, and I thought—this is the most beautiful baby I have ever seen. Maybe I'm less than objective when I talk about Nat's poems. But I don't think so.

I've always resisted the notion that artists need to suffer in order to write. It's a foolish and dangerous notion because, let's face it: even the happiest or luckiest life is fraught with sorrow. Nobody gets out of life alive. Or as the Greeks like to put it, "Count no man happy till he's dead and buried."

Artists don't have a corner on suffering. And they don't need to engineer their own disasters in order to feed the poetry machine. Life is more than generous in that department.

No, artists are artists because they make art; and just like the rest of us, they suffer only because they're human. But that said, I do think art is inconceivable without a world of pain and struggle; art arises, in part, as a response to suffering, even if suffering alone isn't quite enough to turn anyone into Mozart or Picasso. If scientists ever found a cure for aging and death, I think we poets would be out of business. I think we'd all live like the hypothetical lovers in Andrew Marvell's "To His Coy Mistress," devoting thousands upon thousands of years to courtship and foreplay. We'd be like the gods who do mess around with art, that's true, but only because they envy us our hard-earned excellence, our skill, our ability to work creatively within the inescapable limitations of time and space, of gravity, death, and loss. The gods have no capacity for excellence, no real talent, aesthetic or otherwise, because they're limitless beings. When LeBron James leaps from the foul line and dunks the ball with one hand, we watch in amazement because he's redefined what we thought was possible within the rules of the game and the physical laws of the universe. When Apollo does it, we say: So what? Big deal, he's just a god.

Nearly twenty-five hundred years ago, Aeschylus wrote that suffering is our best and most reliable teacher. The well-wadded stupidity that insulates us most of the time wears thin in times of crisis, and we are hurt into deeper levels of awareness; we see more keenly into the mystery of things. If nothing else, suffering (the heart that has to break to change, to open) teaches us the value of not suffering, and it makes us painfully aware of the fragility and evanescence of everything we love. In *The Republic*, Plato says that the pathos of tragedy speaks to a part of the soul that is by nature predisposed to weep for itself. In other words, we're hardwired to want representations of unhappiness. Aeschylus and Plato and every writer since would have understood down to their very nerve ends exactly what Nat means when he writes, "My tears see more than my eyes."

Where there is suffering, which is to say, where there is human life, there is art. But art doesn't merely mirror the bad things that happen to us. It shapes what happens into meaning. And there is always great joy and pleasure, even happiness, in the fundamental human act of shaping. It's not, as Plato believed, that some part of the soul desires to weep for itself; it's rather that the soul possesses a stubborn need for pleasure; it urgently desires to convert weeping into laughter, the sorrow of subject matter into the satisfaction of form. It is a uniquely human instinct—to bring the greatest degree of childlike exuberant playfulness to bear upon the harshest and most difficult realities, answering the tragic gravity of life with the comedic grace of imaginative transformation, shaping life into a vitally clarifying or comprehending image of itself.

In his poems, Nat confronts his situation and also resists it or momentarily transcends it. He becomes a maker, not just a sufferer. He turns his suffering into an occasion for play. I can't read his poems and not feel an animating joy. His poetry, like all good poetry, despite how grim or sorrowful it is, projects and affirms an image of human flourishing. He may write about extreme depression, but there's nothing depressed about the writing. In his poems he may even say he wants to die, but the vitality with which he says this contradicts the very thing he says. One could make the same claim about Sylvia Plath's last poems, or any good work about despair. Writing a good poem about how bad you feel doesn't protect you from that feeling or release you from it. But the mental energy that Nat's poetry embodies and enacts is healthy, life affirming (whatever else may be at work inside him)—and not just for the writer, or the desperate son, but for the reader, too, the desperate, if hopeful, father.

Translation as "Linguistic Hospitality"

A few years ago, a couple from Bulgaria spent a summer house sitting for a family in my neighborhood. They brought with them a two-year-old Bulgarian sheepdog named Pieron. I met them on the street while walking my dog Jelly, a four-year-old pound dog. Their English was spotty at best, and my Bulgarian nonexistent. I asked them how they were settling in, and the couple smiled and nodded vigorously in agreement with whatever it was they thought I'd asked. I then asked what brought them to the States, but thinking maybe I had inquired about their dog and whether he was house trained, they pointed to Pieron and pantomimed some sort of squatting action. They asked me something, gesturing toward the street and the houses on it, which I took to mean they wanted to know if the neighborhood was safe, and I said we hadn't had many break-ins (I mimed someone smashing a window), and they must have thought I said something about dog training and the need for tough love because the woman said, "No no, no no," and in a gentle tone said something to Pieron that made him lie down and roll over.

The dogs, on the other hand, had no trouble communicating. By way of introduction, they wagged their tails, they panted and whimpered, they sniffed and licked each other in the usual places, and then, having broken the ice, like instant pals, chums for life, they chased each other happily in a circle, one of them stopping every now and then to pee on a bush, which the other promptly inspected, approved of, and added a few of his own drops to before running on. It didn't matter what language their masters spoke, where they came from, or how long they'd been in the United States. It didn't matter if their pack was large or small, kibbutzlike or suburban nuclear. It didn't matter if their owners were a mixed-race couple, heterosexual, gay, or married. No linguistic or cultural differences got in the way of understanding. From the first sniff, they communicated perfectly. It wouldn't have mattered if my dog had been a great Dane and theirs had been a pug or a chihuahua, unless of course we wanted to breed them (imagine that!), but even then I'm sure something could have been worked out. Theirs was and is a pre-Babel world, a world of pure denotation without any connotation or subtext that might impede communication, a world governed by a single, biologically established universal canine Esperanto, requiring no translation. Or as Auden put it in his sonnet sequence "In Time of War," "Their hour of birth, their only time at college."

But we, their incoherent, haplessly gesticulating, socially and culturally constructed masters, we are definitely post-Babel. The traces of whatever perfect Ur-Edenic-lingua-franca tongue we may have spoken when we came down from the trees to hunt and gather on two legs across the hot savannah have long since vanished from the earth.

One might argue that we are post-Babel even within the languages we speak. If we think of the subjective life of sensation and emotion, and even thought to some extent, as prelinguistic and internal, then to speak or write or read about that inner life is to go beyond it; it is, in a way, to translate the subjectively primary, the immediate, into the linguistically and socially established forms of communication and expression, to the alteration of both by their conformity to each other—personal experience particularizes those predetermined and thus impersonal conventions of expression, while those conventions in turn socialize or make accessible the privacy of feeling. Don't we also turn what someone writes or tells us into "other words" in order to demonstrate our understanding—"Oh, so what you're saying is that this isn't a poem about the 1978 NBA finals between Philadelphia and Portland but a poem about dental hygiene in twelfth-century France." "In other words": we translate into other words as a way to show we understand. Paul Ricoeur refers to this as internal translation (translation between speakers of the same language). And if something is always lost in translation even between speakers of the same language, as it surely is (just ask anyone who's been married for more than a month), imagine how much harder and trickier it is to translate, externally, from language to language, much less from poetry to poetry.

When I took on the project of translating *The Oresteia*, I faced an even harder task than this, for the highly stylized poetry of ancient Greek tragedy employs a weird composite dialect which, as John Herrington has written, "was never spoken outside the theater but was mostly as remote from the language of the streets as the tragic masks and costumes were from the dress of the streets." Add to that the richness and variety of Aeschylus's quantitative meters, his verbal, metaphorical density, and the links in tragic poetry of particular meters with particular modes of discourse and levels of feeling, and you can see how overmatched I felt. My ambition as translator wasn't just to translate word for word from ancient Greek to contemporary English, but to translate the poetry of ancient Greek into a credible, living poetry in English. I could see an infinite number of ways of doing this badly but no way of doing it well.

I felt, in fact, a little like Orestes himself. Caught between equally bad alternatives, Orestes, I remind myself, is unable to act without incurring someone's wrath: either he offends Apollo if he doesn't avenge his father's murder by killing his mother, or he offends the Erinyes, the furies, protectors of blood kin, if he kills his mother to appease his father. He can't act without betraying someone.

I too felt caught in a double bind. I could be faithful to the ancient Greek and betray my mother tongue; or I could keep faith with the poetry of my own language as it's practiced now and produce actable or sayable verses that betray the complex, strange semantic and musical vitality of the ancient original. In trying to accommodate the profound otherness of ancient tragedy word for word, sentence for sentence, I risk producing verses you couldn't imagine anyone ever saying in English, on or off the stage, at least not with a straight face; but in domesticating that foreign style into idiomatic English, in making it too familiar, I risk displacing the conventions of another poetry with the poetic conventions and values of our particular moment, which wouldn't be translation at all but a kind of literary narcissism masquerading as translation.

My job "in other words" was to make the strange familiar, but not too much so, and the familiar strange, but not too much so, a precarious balancing act that Paul Ricoeur describes as "linguistic hospitality."

Hospitality is an attractive and insightful metaphor on many counts. It assumes that all communication involves a reciprocal welcoming, or opening of the other to ourselves even while we open ourselves to the other. When we translate, we are both host and guest: we simultaneously inhabit the other's words in their linguistic home and receive the other's words into our own. What makes a good host or a good guest is both a respect for difference, since no two languages are ever perfectly reducible to one another, and a recognition that difference itself is less a problem to be overcome by communication than the very condition within which communication takes place. The metaphor assumes translation is at best a rough, always imperfect approximation, not a perfect re-creation. It encourages not the arrogance of appropriation, replacing the original with a version of ourselves or replacing ourselves with a version of the original, but mutual deference, mutual accommodation. Its goal is not to naturalize the words of the other but to make them creditably accessible in their very strangeness, which in turn will sensitize us to the strangeness and limitations of our own mother tongue. It cautions us to be respectful hosts and guests by graciously acknowledging that in an after-Babel world translation is a necessary, unavoidable, but imperfect enterprise and that no translation, not even Chapman's Homer, is or ever could be permanent.

No translation can ever escape the history of style, the partiality and finitude of its linguistic moment. And sooner or later, even the most brilliant renderings will be replaced by other renderings more or less finite, more or less flawed, more or less brilliant. Each generation dresses the classic texts up in its own clothes—and a change in style requires a change of wardrobe. Chapman's Homer in heptameter couplets was replaced by Pope's Homer in heroic couplets, which in the more informal twentieth century has been replaced by Lattimore's loose six-beat blank hexameter, or Fitzgerald's blank verse, or Fagles's or Logue's free verse. Whereas a poet aspires to a kind of immortality, writing for the ages and all that, a translator should consider himself lucky if his work lasts a generation. Like a good guest, he knows not to overstay his welcome.

If all translation is after Babel, and thus imperfect and temporary, how do we distinguish a good one from a bad one? What standards do we use? If failure and betrayal are inevitable, how much is too much? How do we fail and betray in interesting and illuminating ways, in ways that make the translation itself an act of intimate appreciation and understanding of the original's unique achievement?

Here are three versions of the opening lines of the *Oresteia* that illustrate some of the risks and pitfalls I've been discussing abstractly; I'll use the model of hospitality to explain and, to some extent, evaluate the differences. The first version is Robert Browning's:

The gods I ask deliverance from these labours,
Watch of a year's length whereby, slumbering through it
On the Atreidai's roofs on elbow,—dog-like—
I know of nightly star-groups the assemblage,
And those that bring to men winter and summer
Bright dynasts, as they pride them in the aether.
—Stars, when they wither, and the uprisings of them.
And now on ward I wait the torch's token,
The glow of fire, shall bring from Troia message
And word of capture; so prevails audacious
The man's-way-planning hoping heart of woman.
But when I, driven from night-rest, dew-drenched hold to
This couch of mine—not looked upon by visions,
Since fear instead of sleep still stands beside me,
So as that fast I fix in sleep no eyelids—
And when to sing or chirp a tune I fancy,

For slumber such song-remedy infusing,
I wail then, for this House's fortune groaning,
Not, as of old, after the best ways governed.
Now, lucky be deliverance from these labours,
At good news—the appearing dusky fire!
O hail, thou lamp of night, a day-long lightness
Revealing, and of dances the ordainment!
Halloo, halloo!
To Agamemnon's wife I show, by shouting,
That, from bed starting up at once, I' the household
Joyous acclaim, good-omened to this torch-blaze,
She send aloft, if haply Ilion's city
Be taken, as the beacon boasts announcing.
Ay, and, for me, myself, will dance a prelude,
For, that my master's dice drop right, I'll reckon:
Since thrice-six has it thrown to me, this signal.
Well, may it hap that, as he comes, the loved hand
O' the household's lord I may sustain with this hand!
As for the rest, I'm mute: on tongue a big ox
Has trodden. Yet this House, if voice it take should,
Most plain would speak. So, willing I myself speak
To those who know: to who know not—I'm blankness.

In a preface to the translation, Browning declares that his ambition was "to reproduce the very turn of each Greek phrase in as Greek a fashion as English will bear." He boasts that he adhered to the literal meaning and phraseology at every cost save "actual violence to the language." We'll get to that issue in a moment. The first thing to notice is the meter: Browning substitutes blank verse (iambic pentameter) for the Greek hexameter line. He clearly isn't comfortable dispensing with rhyme for fear perhaps that the lines would lack a suitable formality without it, so he enjambs very little, and then ends each line with an unaccented syllable (a feminine ending), the way, for instance, Leonard Cohen does in his famous song "Suzanne": "Suzanne takes you down to her place near the river / . . . she feeds you tea and oranges / That come all the way from China." In Browning's translation, the feminine endings and the end stopping make the lines move stiffly, like a Frankensteinian march of iambs; they read like rhyming lines in which the rhymes failed to show up. Adding the extra unaccented syllable to the pentameter may also represent an attempt to allude to the Greek hexameter, to give a hexameter feel to otherwise pentameter lines.

Beyond the stilted versification, what stands out in Browning's version is the warped and twisted syntax and the inverted phrases ("of nightly star-groups the assemblage" and "fast I fix in sleep no eyelids"). The distance between his English and an English you could imagine anybody of any era ever saying is absolute. Browning honors the Aeschylean compound epithets: "so prevails audacious / The man's-way-planning hoping heart of woman"—this is as close to the original Greek as one could come and still speak English, but in so doing he sounds unintentionally comic, like the Lite Beer from Miller commercials that ran a few years back, the ones that celebrated the unsung heroes of our culture: "Here's to you, Mr. Towel-wiping-the-sweat-off-of-the-benches-in-the-men's-locker-room-after-the-men-have-showered-and-gone-home-to-dinner Guy." He's also like the British Francophile that Ben Jonson satirizes in his "On English Monsieur": "That he, untraveled, should be French so much / As Frenchmen in his company should seem Dutch?"

My favorite moment in Browning's version of the watchman's speech comes toward the end, when the watchman imagines how plainly and straightforwardly the house would speak if it were free to: "Yet this house, if voice it take should, / most plain would speak." The inversion of "take should" for "should take" is dictated not by the original text but by Browning's desire to end each line with an unaccented syllable. The normal word order would have broken the pattern, so goodbye normal word order, hello "take should"—a wonderful example of the tail wagging the dog.

Before you think that maybe late-nineteenth-century English readers of poetry were more tolerant than twenty-first-century American readers are of inversions, compound epithets, mixed metaphors, and periphrastic diction, take a look at E. A. Housman's parody of Browning's translation in his "Fragment of Greek Tragedy":

Chorus: O suitably-attired-leather-boots
Head of a traveler, wherefore seeking whom
Whence by what way how purposed art thou come
To this well-nightingaled vicinity?
My object in inquiring is to know.
But if you happen to be deaf and dumb
And do not understand a word I say,
Then wave your hand, to signify as much.
Alcmaeon: I journeyed hither a Boetian road.
Chorus: Sailing on horseback, or with feet for oars?
Alcmaeon: Plying with speed my partnership of legs.
Chorus: Beneath a shining or a rainy Zeus?
Alcmaeon: Mud's sister, not himself, adorns my shoes.

Housman does to Browning what Tina Fey did to Sarah Palin during the presidential election—with only slight exaggeration, Housman's mimicking of Browning is impeccable. "Mud's sister," by the way, is dust.

Browning gives us what in the preface to John Denham's 1656 translation of Virgil, *The Destruction of Troy*, Denham calls "a verbal translation." This is a risky enterprise at best, because, as Denham says, "whosoever offers a Verbal Translation shall have the misfortune of that young traveler, who lost his own language abroad and brought home no other instead of it; for the grace of the [Greek] will be lost by being turned into English words; and the grace of the English by being turned into the [Greek] phrase." Browning demonstrates the hazards of a noble ambition: he turns tragedy into slapstick by refusing to settle for what Paul Ricoeur calls "correspondence without complete adhesion," or equivalence without identity.

If Browning oversteps by bringing too much Greek into his English, Fagles's 1996 version of the same lines maybe sacrifices too much of the strange vitality of the original Greek in the name of "realism," his commitment to using a demotic idiom all of us recognize and could imagine speaking on a stage, if not saying on a street:

Dear gods, set me free from all the pain,
The long watch I keep, one whole year awake . . .
Propped on my arms, crouched on the roofs of Atreus
Like a dog.
I know the stars by heart,
The armies of the night, and there in the lead
The ones that bring us snow or the crops of summer,
Bring us all we have—
Our great blazing kings of the sky,
I know them, when they rise and when they fall . . .
And now I watch for the light, the signal-fire
Breaking out of Troy, shouting Troy is taken.

So she commands, full of her high hopes.
That woman—she maneuvers like a man.

While there are stray lines of iambic pentameter and a loose
five-beat accentual meter, Fagles's measure for the speeches as
well as for the odes is free verse. His language is straightforward, colloquial. An uneducated sentry isn't likely to employ
highfalutin diction or overly complicated syntax. Fagles
breaks down certain compound phrases, so frequent in the
original and so unnatural in English, into simple units. So
Clytemnestra's "man-counseling-ever-hopeful-heart" becomes
two short sentences: "So she commands, full of her high hopes. /
That woman—she maneuvers like a man." On the other hand,
if Fagles cultivates a more convincing idiom, an idiom closer
to a speaking voice, he risks flatness and monotony. The short
unvarying phrases after a while sound more like a telegraph
than someone speaking: "Fire all the way." Stop. "I'm for the
morning dances." Stop. "Master's luck is mine." Stop. Finally,
Fagles uses a shorter but phrasal free verse for the odes. And to
my ear they are indistinguishable from the speeches, maybe a
bit more imagistic but musically hard to tell apart. Browning,
on the other hand, employs rhyme as well as meter for the odes,
which does mark them off from the speeches and the sticho-
mythia, the alternating lines of dialogue. Unfortunately, the
syntactical distortions in his odes are even more egregious.

The third version of the Watchman's speech is mine. I
tried to steer a middle course between these two extremes. I
wanted the verse to sound like verse at all times, and I wanted
to maintain a clear and audible distinction between the verse
that speaks and the verse that sings. I also wanted to strike a
tone more elevated than normal English without ceasing to

be English. By using free verse for the speeches and dialogue, Fagles achieves a degree of immediacy and directness as well as readability that is often quite effective. But his free verse often sounds like lineated prose, and it's incapable of modulating into higher registers of feeling the way blank verse can. Blank verse is a much more flexible instrument: it can modulate upward or downward, between formal and informal levels of speech; it can be adapted to almost any voice, any character, any mood. It provides a wider range of possibilities than free verse can, at least in Fagles's hands.

But there's a more important reason why I chose a finely articulated meter for my translation of *Oresteia*. Broadly speaking, the trilogy is about justice as a sort of cosmic balance that inevitably and inexorably rights itself both by means of *and* despite the evil deeds of characters who claim to act on justice's behalf. If justice is an eternal norm, then unjust human action is a distortion of or departure from the norm. It is the norm itself, however, that defines the distortion as distortion, that measures the extent of the departure. In a sense, this cosmic justice is never more present or active than when it's being warped by some particularly evil act and then invoked to justify that evil. This tension between norm and variation on the metaphysical level is echoed in the tension on the metrical level between the underlying but ever-recurring norm of the iambic cadence, the metrical grid, and the rhythmical variations playing constantly around it, variations that the norm itself makes audible as expressive variations even as the variations modify our perception of that norm, muting it at one moment, emphasizing it the next. Since the Aeschylean universe operates on principles consistent with the principles of metrical composition, I felt that the most hospitable way to do "justice" to the *Oresteia* was to cast the trilogy in a clear but flexible accentual-

syllabic line, a line in which repetition and surprise, norm
and variation were constantly in play, constantly resisting and
defining one another, each becoming what it is, working its own
destiny out, in and through its relation to the other.

Here are the opening lines of my version:

WATCHMAN: I beg the gods to deliver me at last
from this hard watch I've kept now for a year
upon the palace roof of the Atreidae,
dog-like, snout to paws, night after long
night, studying the congress of the stars,
the unignorable bright potentates
that bring down through the night sky to us here
below, the summer now, and now the winter,
eternal even as they wane and rise.

I try to keep the blank verse limber by doing several things: I
occasionally substitute trochaic and anapestic feet for the normative iamb, and in lines that contain no substitutions, I vary
the degree of stress among accented and unaccented syllables
while maintaining the iambic cadence—"to rise from her soft
bed and raise a shout"; I often play the grammatical phrases
off against the metrical feet, so that pauses within the lines
fall sometimes between feet and sometimes within them, and
I shift the caesura (the internal line pause) to different positions within the line by varying the lengths of the enjambed
clauses. At the same time, I make the lines cut into the sentences at relatively stable places so that the metrical norm
remains audible even as its audibility modulates from line to
line. For example, lines 15–16: "by night, and damp with dew
by morning, and / Just fear (no dream or sleep) comes near it."
I do, "in other words," what all poets writing in English do when

they try to write expressive blank verse lines: they channel William Shakespeare, John Milton, William Wordsworth, Browning himself in his own poems, and Wallace Stevens, the poets who have helped refine blank verse into the supple instrument it is or can be in the right hands under the right circumstances.

Like Browning, I wanted to preserve some sense of Aeschylus's weird compacted diction and imagery but without resorting to absurdly mixed metaphors and turns of phrase that no one in her right mind would ever dream of saying. I can illustrate how hard it was to do this by looking at one particular metaphor that comes early in the parados (the introductory choral ode) at line 140. In the original, lion cubs are described as dewdrops of ferocious lions. This metaphor just doesn't work in English; it conveys the idea of how something dangerous can grow out of something that seems harmless and lovely, but it's too soft and sickly, more like a Swinburnian venereal disease than a lion cub. Fagles sensibly avoids the metaphor altogether, translating the phrase as "ravening lion's tender." Ever faithful to the Greek, Browning writes, "those dew drop things fierce lions whelp." I try to gesture in the direction of the metaphor while at the same time steering clear of it, saying, "the dew slick cubs of ferocious lions." Where I decide to abandon metaphors, I still attempt to insinuate them, and I refuse to throw them aside in favor of abstractions. In keeping with the metaphorical spirit, I try to keep the language as concrete as I can.

My diction is thinner than Browning's, but thicker than Fagles's, but not nearly as rich and intricate as Aeschylus's. There is simply no way to bring his complex music over into English. The amalgamation of lyric meters Aeschylus incorporates into tragedy, each with its own particular conventions and tonal associations, is impossible to replicate. All the translator can hope to do is give some flavor of the original, or find some metrical or stylistic analogies for untranslatable metrical effects. All that a translator can do is offer an intimate and creative reading in his own language of the original, a reading that reveals and even honors the unique richness of the primary text in and through its very failure to reproduce it. Like Fagles and Browning, and every translator in every language who has ever taken on the *Oresteia*, I have failed to do it justice, though in ways that I hope will cause a reader to see how unsurpassable the original is, and sensitize her to what her own linguistic and literary conventions can and cannot do.

Cervantes says that reading a translation, no matter how good it is, is like "looking at the Flanders tapestries from behind: you can see the basic shapes but they're so filled with threads that you cannot fathom their original lustre." The basic shapes, the general meaning, the plot, all of that we can reproduce. But the original luster, the magnificent dense texture of a foreign poetry, the intricately connotative web of idioms and forms—that can't possibly be duplicated. And maybe we shouldn't want it to be. Out of the respect for our linguistic guest, we shouldn't try to pass ourselves off as "one of them" but accept our differences as the very means by which we try to meet as best we can. To switch metaphors, maybe the best we can hope for is a linguistic version of margarine: no matter how good it is or what we call it (I Can't Believe It's Not Aeschylus), we're still left, as we should be, with a hankering for the real thing.

Coda

I want to conclude by briefly examining some of the implications of Ricoeur's metaphor of hospitality for the writing of original work. What does it mean to think of yourself as the host of your mother tongue instead of merely the wielder of it? In one sense, experience becomes primarily linguistic. That is, as hosts of our mother tongue, we are ultimately accountable to the language itself. But because hospitality also presupposes social exchange in which host and guest attempt to conform to norms of social behavior, the metaphor highlights the inescapably conventional or social nature of expression. This goes back to my earlier comment about the creative tension between subjective experience and the socially or linguistically established conventions by which that experience is conveyed and understood. In this metaphor, originality isn't at odds with convention but dependent on it, in the same way that our experience of rhythmical variation in a poem depends on some established pattern or form, some expectation of recurrence. Without an expectation of recurrence, there's nothing to vary from. When I write a personal lyric in, say, a highly enjambed free verse line, I am inviting into the poem the poets who have bequeathed to me that form for my present use, who invented and refined it and made it possible for me to speak as I do. If the poem is good, my voice is changed by theirs, broadened and deepened beyond its immediate moment (even if the immediate moment is its concern); and their voices, too, are changed by mine by being brought back to life in a different time and place (in what, for them, would be foreign circumstances). They are translated forward into the present just they translate me back into the past.

As host, one entertains (in the radical sense of the word) not the language as an abstract entity but the language as a living and ever-changing force of social meaning. I think this quality of hospitality is what makes Browning, for instance, such a superb translator *within* the English language in his own poems. In his dramatic monologues, he is exquisitely alert to the way complex emotional and psychological points of view express themselves in the very conventions they often try to hide behind, or the way competing perspectives impede the very communication they necessitate.

In "Andrea del Sarto," for instance, consider the utter complexity of the painter's emotional situation and the stylistic equivalents Browning finds for that complexity: the way recurrent images of gold convey the painter's pride and shame, in relation to both work and love, and of gray for resignation and failure, or the way the halting, constantly qualifying sentences that reverse themselves midthought and then reverse the reversals, or peter out in ellipses, capture the speaker's paralyzing ambivalence toward his wife, himself, his art, his helpless dependence on a woman whom he nonetheless resents, his inability to silence that resentment or to speak of it too directly for fear of driving her away; his love and hatred of Lucrezia's "perfect beauty," which mirrors both the pride he takes in the technical perfection of his paintings and the withering, self-abasing sense that technical ability divorced from spiritual reach is worse than nothing. At one point in the poem, Browning catches del Sarto in the act of translating his self-deceived, self-justifying words into a language that Lucrezia with her merely mercenary interest in his art could understand: "if you would sit thus by me every night / I should work better, do you comprehend? / I mean that I should earn more, give you more."

In "My Last Duchess," Browning translates the Duke's psychotic jealousy and haughty self-justifying pride into images and metaphors that bring his dark subjectivity into vivid focus. The curtain that veils the painting of his late wife, and that he alone can pull back for the viewer, the statue of Neptune taming a sea horse, and the long sentences that the couplets can't contain provide a wonderfully precise equivalent of the Duke's insane possessiveness and rampant egotism. At one point in the poem, Browning shows the Duke attempting to translate the language of greed into the language of love, or something like love, yet in such a way that only reveals the greed more starkly:

> The count your master's known munificence
> Is ample warrant that no just pretense
> of mine for dowry will be disallowed,
> though his fair daughter's self, as I avowed
> at starting, is my object.

Catching himself expressing too explicitly his expectation of an ample dowry, the Duke turns midsentence away from the mention of money to the count's fair daughter, yet the turn itself only intensifies the very possessiveness it may or may not be covering up—the girl, he says, is his object, a word that chillingly reminds us of what the Duke appears to be trying not to say, that he has no "feeling" for this girl, that all she really is to him is an object, because that's all he is, a collector of objects. The very shape of this sentence, too, reinforces the depth and passion of his arrogance and self-aggrandizement: despite what the Duke avows, we can't forget that he places the monetary impulse in the main clause, and the conventional sentiment (the count's fair daughter's self) in the subordinate clause, as if the sentimental impulse were an afterthought, which, of course, for him it is. Either the Duke trips up inadvertently and then attempts to cover his tracks, or, perhaps more interestingly, he trips up on purpose, acknowledging the conventional sentiment only superficially by means of the concessive clause ("though his fair daughter's self") in order to demonstrate his arrogant freedom from the conventions everyone but he with his nine-hundred-year-old name must live by. Either way, the Duke (and Browning, through the Duke) is translating for us an unconventional character by means of conventions we understand.

In the same preface I quoted earlier, John Denham says that there are "certain graces and happinesses peculiar to every language, which give life and energy to the words." This of course is what makes translation so difficult and requires of the translator that she transform the text imaginatively in order to honor it, not simply translate it word for word. As Browning's botched translation of the *Oresteia* demonstrates, you can't expect to carry over those identical graces and happinesses without doing violence to your language and the language you're translating from. One could argue that the genius of Browning's dramatic monologues is the application of this idea—that every language possesses virtues peculiar to itself—to each and every character, psychic state, perspective, and moment of experience he generously, nonjudgmentally, inhabits. In Browning's poems, each particular psychic/social state or predicament generates its own particular linguistic equivalent. This is what makes communication between his speakers necessary and difficult. What is this but a problem of translation? With generous particularity on every stylistic level, sonic and semantic, Browning entertains points of view that refuse to entertain each other. In this respect, in these poems, if not in his translations proper, he exemplifies the translator at his creative, most hospitable best.

Some Questions Concerning
Art and Suffering

In the fall of 1999, my brother was dying of brain cancer, my marriage was falling apart, and I had just moved into the basement apartment of a house whose owner was an eighty-five-year-old woman with Alzheimer's disease who every few days would knock on my door and introduce herself. One night in the middle of this outtake from the book of Job, I had a dream in which *The Oresteia* by Aeschylus, which I was translating at the time, had been adapted for *The Jerry Springer Show*. What I remember mostly are the characters as they came on stage: Agamemnon first—decked out in armor, spear in hand, horsehair bobbing from his helmet: as he strides to his chair, the caption on the screen reads: Sacrificed Daughter to Stop Wind! He's followed by Cassandra, who staggers out, babbling incoherently. The caption flashes: *Thinks* she's clairvoyant! Then Oedipus, not Clytemnestra, strides confidently to his seat, so confident in fact that he hasn't noticed that he's strayed in off the set of another tragedy, while Jerry whispers to the home audience, "Slept with mother, murdered father, doesn't realize it yet!"

At this point the dream gets really bizarre. Clytemnestra shows up next with Aegisthus in tow. She's dressed in fishnet stockings and a bowtie, he's wearing tennis whites. Agamemnon lunges for Clytemnestra, and in the melee he is stabbed to death. Aegisthus, now standing over Agamemnon's ravaged body, pulls out a copy of *Idylls of the King* and asks, Tennyson anyone? Then as Agamemnon's wrapped up in a red carpet and carried off, the audience isn't chanting JER-RY, JER-RY, JER-RY, as they usually do, but DI-KE, DI-KE, DI-KE (the Greek word for justice)!

OK, so it wasn't a dream. I made the whole thing up. But if I'd had such a dream around that time, I would have wakened from it feeling purged if not of all my fear and pity, then of any sense that Greek tragedy or art of any kind could have consoled me for my troubles or made the pain of what I had to face more bearable.

Which is not to say that I don't love the *Oresteia*. Or that translating it at that particular time, in the midst of so much turmoil, wasn't one of the great joys of my writing life. In fact, while I found it difficult to write my own poetry during this awful year, I had no trouble whatsoever working obsessively on the trilogy. I worked on it at home when I could, I worked on it between classes, I worked on it at the hospital in any number of waiting rooms while my brother had this or that procedure done. I even worked on it in my lawyer's office just after my wife and I split up, a month or so before my brother died.

In one of his letters, John Keats remarks that in times of difficulty the objects of desire become a refuge as well as a passion. This was certainly true for me, though what does it say about *my* difficulties that I would seek refuge from them in the House of Atreus: what kind of person goes to the House of Atreus for a little R&R? The challenge of translating the richness and complexity of Aeschylus's language into a poetically charged but sayable English that was still faithful to the original Greek did indeed distract me from the pain that I was living through. It was like a monumental puzzle I could play with endlessly. It kept me hugely entertained, became a source of inexhaustible pleasure at a time when life seemed nothing but a vale of tears.

I would like to say that working on the *Oresteia* at this particular time was more than a distraction, more than just a sensational escape from the shapeless sorrows of real life. For what I was living with and thinking about and puzzling over was a story depicting human beings in desperate situations, which (you would think) couldn't help but resonate with what I myself was going through. While the stylization of the language, the historical remoteness of the story, the dramatic conventions peculiar to another age, another culture all insisted that this was not my story, the human drama itself and the portrayal of people caught in the toils of necessity, attempting to find some justification for all they do and suffer, insisted that I sympathize with them and think about the moral problems that their lives embody. I didn't do this, though, however much I expected to or wanted to. At least not in any way that changed me, or blunted the pain of my family circumstances, or made those circumstances more endurable or meaningful. If there was consolation in the *Oresteia*, maybe that consolation had only to do with learning all about a family more dysfunctional than mine.

In any event, forget catharsis. Forget clarity. If nothing else, what translating the *Oresteia* gave me was respite from an unbearable experience, which, precisely for the brief respite, seemed all the more unbearable when the respite was over.

The great pleasure I got from doing this work was partly a function of the distance between the world of the play and the messy particulars of everyday existence. A drama that dealt with human suffering in a more contemporary setting, that reflected my own circumstances too directly, might not have pleased me nearly as much. In fact, one of the unstated rules of Greek tragedy is that there be significant distance between the experience of the audience and the characters on stage, that the drama not engage the audience's personal circumstances too transparently. Phrynichus, a contemporary of Aeschylus, learned this the hard way. He produced a play about the Persian slaughter of the Milesians, a disaster that had devastated the Athenians, who were deeply partisan to the Milesian cause. The tragedy cut too close to home. The Athenians were so upset by the play that according to Herodotus they required Phrynichus to pay a stiff fine and passed a law forbidding anyone ever to stage this play again. The moral seems to be that it's better to show us someone else's troubles than our own, which reminds me of the joke about the old Jew on his deathbed who converts to Catholicism: when the priest asks him why, he answers, "Better one of you should die than one of us."

"It is certain," Hume tells us in *Of Tragedy*, "that the same object of distress which pleases in tragedy, were it really set before us, would give the most unfeigned uneasiness." In any representation of suffering, some degree of distance is required if the suffering is to be transformed into aesthetic pleasure.

But now I wonder, why represent suffering at all? As the Herald asks in *Agamemnon*, the first play of the *Oresteia*, "Why must I tell the tale of all the lost, / and why should the living live it through again / in stories, groaning over old misfortune?" He does tell the tale, of course, at great length and beautifully. In fact, so beautifully that the answer to his question is implicit in the telling of his story: the living live through old misfortune again because it feels good to do so. The Herald relishes the telling, and the chorus (as do we) eats it up. We all crave stories about terrible things happening to other people, bad people, good people, especially people who, like us, don't deserve to suffer as they do.

But to say that we're eager to hear about the hard lives of other people is still not to answer the question *why?* Why do we get pleasure from artistic representations of pain? And what is the nature of that pleasure? How does poetry or any art convert intractable sorrow into aesthetic joy that at the same time respects and even honors that intractability, without reducing pain to spectacle? How does it make attractive what we would turn away from in disgust if it were truly happening right in front of us? Distance may be part of the answer, but only part. How does art do this without falsifying or minimizing the harshness of the realities it's attempting to express and understand?

There are all kinds of answers to these questions, many of them true to some extent, none of them entirely satisfying. Good poems about misfortune please us by making us feel less alone; they console us by connecting us to others who have suffered what we've suffered or whose suffering reminds us of our frailties, our own helplessness—in this connection think of the opening scene of Sophocles's *Aias*, in which Athena puts the reluctant Odysseus in the position of an audience member, forcing him to watch and listen to the still-deluded, bloodstained Aias recount his disgraceful rampage of the night before, slaughtering cattle he mistook for the leaders of the Achaean army. Odysseus responds the way, I think, we are all meant to respond to tragic suffering: his first impulse is to avert his gaze, then he feels pity (even for his enemy), and pity in turn leads him to the recognition that "the same fate could be mine: we who live are all phantoms, fleeting shadows."

Good poems about misfortune also flatter us by encouraging us to sympathize with people different from ourselves, and thus they make us feel less self-absorbed; they free us from our fears and anxieties by giving vent to them; they make us more keenly aware of how precious life is by reminding us of life's fragility (or as Joni Mitchell says, "Don't it always seem to go that you don't know what you've got till it's gone?"). By converting irremediable loss, heartbreak, physical or spiritual despair into something beautiful, good poems about bad things make us feel less helpless in the face of what we can't control. And at least while we read them, good poems that wrest aesthetic pleasure from bereavement and misery make us feel triumphant, even when the sense of triumph emanates from lines that tell us that defeat is unavoidable.

The operative word, of course, is *good*. Bad poems too can make us feel less alone, or be cathartic, or remind us of our vulnerabilities. Sentimental melodrama can elicit the "fearful horror and tearful pity and doleful yearnings" that Gorgias, the fifth-century teacher of rhetoric, considered the typical effects of poetry at its best. They can do all the things that good poems do and yet still fail to give the essential and enduring pleasure good poems give. That essential and enduring pleasure can only come through artistry. This is what Yeats means when he says that "neither scholars nor populace have sung or read anything generation after generation because of its pain. Imagination must dance, must be carried beyond feeling into aboriginal ice." Art as well as distance (or should I say art that is itself a function of distance) is essential to the transformation of suffering into aesthetic pleasure.

To say this, though, is not to say that content doesn't matter or that form is everything. In our culture (and I venture to say in all cultures), poems about the darker aspects of existence far outnumber happier works of art. The greatest poems, the masterpieces, are the ones about love lost, not loved gained, about deserved or undeserved bad luck, about sorrow, not joy—or if joy, then joy recollected in a time of sorrow (and so thereby becoming another source of pain). The best poems confront the most difficult things. As Martha Nussbaum reminds us, "Great art plays a central role in our political lives because, showing us the tangled nature of our loves and commitments, showing us ourselves as flawed crystals, it moderates the optimistic hatred of the actual that makes for a great deal of political violence, moderates the ferocious hopefulness that simply marches over the complicated delicacies of the human heart." Content matters. But content is only a necessary but never sufficient element of great art; the other crucial element is the form-giving imagination of the artist. The pleasure ultimately inheres in the artistry. And artistry is itself an act of attention, an act of witnessing that permeates every aspect of the language—the words, the changing shape of sentences, the dance of sentences through and across the lines.

The difference between what we suffer in our daily lives and the suffering enacted in a Greek tragedy has to do with how that suffering is shaped and ordered, and thereby invested with meaning that clarifies the lives depicted and, by extension, our own sense of what it means to be alive. Or as Oliver Taplin puts it, "The tragedies of real life, unlike those of the stage, are often shapeless, sordid, capricious, meaningless. But supposing this to be true (as I do), what then? It is not human to be content with this useless, even if ultimate, truth. We must try to understand, to cope, to respond. It is in this attempt that tragedy— that most great art—has its place."

Bad poems are bad because they witness incompletely. They flinch in the face of crisis, seeking refuge in cliché or platitude, or even in Beauty that falsifies by failing to attend to the beauty-resisting, irreducibly complicated truths of hard experience.

When we read a poem about some catastrophic illness, some devastating loss or terrible injustice, we can truly feel less alone only if the poem honors the complexity of what we didn't know we knew; we can truly feel connected to others, to a community of fellow hostages to fortune, only if the isolating inward force of pain has been countered by the outward social force of language brought to an unforgettable because pervasive state of intense responsiveness.

Or so at least the liberal humanist in me wants desperately to believe. But the postmodern skeptic who watched his sister and brother die so horribly and his family fall apart, and who now can't help but see art as a necessary but woefully inadequate response to suffering and loss, can't give his full assent. I can neither embrace the belief that art redeems our losses nor entirely renounce it. The humanist writer in me honors the *Oresteia* by translating it as faithfully and beautifully as I can. The postmodern skeptic thumbs his nose at all that great, high-minded artistry by imagining one of the cornerstones of Western civilization adapted for *The Jerry Springer Show*.

At the same time, I know that a strain of the same distrust and skepticism runs through the genre itself, and that the best tragedies both appeal to our desire that art redeem or make sense of the terrible things we suffer and acknowledge the improbability of doing so. I'm not suggesting here that tragedy, or art in general, makes nothing happen or serves no purpose beyond itself. Some tragedies do arise in relation to political crises and attempt to keep in play imaginative and moral possibilities that may be threatened by political decisions or events. One can read Euripides's *The Trojan Women* as a plea for compassion made in response to the Athenian decision to slaughter all the men on the Island of Melos and send all the women and children into slavery in punishment for the Melians' refusal to become an ally of Athens in its war with Sparta. The play of course did not avert the atrocity (what work of art ever has?), but it did remind its audience of the humanity of people they were killing and dispossessing. That the atrocity does go forward in the play (as it did in the world of fifth-century Athens, as it does today) in turn reminds us that this is after all only a work of art. What tragedy can do, perhaps better than any other form of art, is to face up to the sheer senseless awfulness of the world without pretending that the art itself makes anything better. If it exalts or affirms the human spirit, it does so by saying that we know what we're up against and we can still live fully in the light of such knowledge. For all the monumental, totalizing claims made on their behalf, the best tragedies recognize the insufficiency of art even as they bring art to the highest level.

This dark but somehow exhilarating aspect of tragedy has shaped the way I think about art and suffering and profoundly influenced the poetry and prose I've written over the past several years. In my book of poems about my brother's death from cancer, *Song and Dance*, I tried to make a monument to my brother, a Broadway performer, a song and dance man; in the spirit of the elegiac tradition, I tried to acknowledge the struggle he endured in his last months and to celebrate his courage. I wrote that book in the weeks and months after his death, in that basement apartment with the demented landlady and while still grieving over the breakup of my own family. People have praised me for the courage it must have taken to write this book; they've remarked upon how lucky I was to have a tool like poetry with which to work through my grief and sorrow, to come to terms with what I've lost. Well, as I wrote those poems, I felt neither courageous nor lucky. While it may have looked from the outside like I was facing my bereavement head on, I was in fact doing just the opposite. Writing was not therapy but the avoidance of therapy; it was not grieving but the avoidance of grief, the deferral of grief, the transformation of what I passively suffered into something I could actively make. I suppose in that sense it was therapeutic. But only in that sense. I was making poems, I was making art. I was transforming an intractable sorrow into an aesthetic problem that the writing of the poems was a way to solve. But all I solved was the writing of the poems. I was not released from pain. And the pain itself, even as I wrote about it, had nothing to do with knowledge; it was only pain. The anger I wrote about did not release me from the anger; I felt no less enraged by the undeserved absurdity and waste of what had happened to my family. If I was happy while I wrote, that's because writing makes me happy, the sheer activity of it, even if what I'm writing about is how unhappy I am.

Only when the book was finished did the miserable, sorrowful day-by-day work of grieving truly begin. The poems themselves continually return to the realization that poetry is only poetry, however much it gives voice to the complexities of the experience, however much it tries confronting pain and making sense of it. The poems remind us that a represented pain is itself an aesthetic pleasure that has little to do with lived pain, that the solace or comfort that comes from giving shape to what we feel doesn't really free us from that feeling, or if it does free us it's only while we read the poem. Hence the title of the book—*Song and Dance*—which refers of course to the fact that my brother was a musical comedy star but also to the pejorative expression "Don't give me that song and dance;" don't try to pull a fast one on me, this isn't going to do what the beauty and grace and formal symmetries suggest it will. I wanted this book to remind the reader at every turn that the division between art and suffering is absolute, even as we still try helplessly to bridge it.

Yes, tragedy does shape and order suffering into monuments of unaging intellect. But monuments estrange us, don't they, from the perishable flesh they mean to honor; they displace the very people they memorialize. The kind of poetry I needed back in 1999, and, frankly, still need now, is one that wants to raise the dead, *literally*, that wants to bring the beloved back to life. It's a poetry that doesn't want to settle for a substitute, however beautiful, a poetry that recognizes the impossibility of what it nonetheless is helpless not to try to do.

One poem that raises if not the dead then many of the questions I've been raising here is "The Beautician" by Thom Gunn, from his great book about the AIDS epidemic, *The Man with Night Sweats*. The plot of the poem is simple. A beautician goes to the morgue to see the body of a dead friend. The friend's hair is all askew, and the beautician, being a beautician, beautifies it:

She, a beautician, came to see her friend
Inside the morgue, when she had had her cry.
She found the body dumped there all awry,
Not as she thought right for a person's end,
Left sideways like that on one arm and thigh.

In their familiarity with the dead
It was as if the men had not been kind
With her old friend, whose hair she was assigned
To fix and shape. She did not speak; instead
She gave her task a concentrated mind.

She did find in it some thin satisfaction
That she could use her tenderness as skill
To make her poor dead friend's hair beautiful

—As if she shaped an epitaph by her action,
She thought—being a beautician after all.

The woman's identity as beautician, or artist, is inversely proportionate to the immediacy of her grief. Only once she has had her private cry can she go to the morgue and carry out the public task assigned to her. It's not that she's no longer grieving when she assumes the role of artist to her dead friend; it's that she isn't merely grieving. She's turning passive grieving into active making, transforming a loss she suffers into an artifact she creates. As she concentrates her mind, she projects that merely personal and isolating grief into the social world of aesthetic action. The key word here is *concentrates*, which means of course to focus, to move in toward the center and thus to narrow, but also, as a function of that narrowing, to intensify.

If the role of artist entails some distance or detachment from the immediacies of private feeling, that distance in turn provides her with a remarkably inclusive vision that is moral as well as aesthetic. As grieving friend, she merely cries. As beautician/friend, she acts, thinks, and imagines in a variety of ways: She thinks about what's right or proper for a person's end. She judges the morgue attendants for the insensitive way they handle her poor friend's corpse. At the same time, she understands how that insensitivity, that coarsening, derives from the nature of their job, from their being perhaps too familiar with the dead.

As beautician, the woman converts her sense of outrage and her own grief into active pleasure. In making her dead friend's hair beautiful, she makes an artifact, a monument, a substitute that memorializes both the friend's existence and the beautician's love. But the satisfaction the beautician takes in doing this is thin, in part because she knows that in memorializing love she is also preserving her grief, her sense of loss, which otherwise would fade, and also, more importantly, because the "epitaph" is no substitute for the person himself. The art is necessary, unavoidable, and at its best inadequate. The epitaph she makes gives pleasure, but the pleasure turns her back to the grief from which it grows.

The epitaph, the work of art, the good poem, heals paradoxically; the distance necessary for memorialization, the distance that enables one to use one's tenderness as skill, the distance needed to create the space for artistic exercise, for forging a social response out of private grief, acknowledges in and through its pleasure and beauty the unredeemable loss and bodily anguish for which no artifact can compensate. The well-chiseled rhyming stanzas of this poem insinuate a monumental, elegiac tradition even while the words, the varying rhythms, the almost offhand rhetorical diffidence of the closing lines ("as if," "she thought," "after all") prevent us from settling too comfortably into the comforts that tradition offers. The pleasure-giving elegiac speech projected out of the grieving body at the same time reminds us of the body's unspeakable suffering.

This is for me the problem with conventional elegy, and with monumentalism in the arts in general: they all insist too smugly on their own importance; the beauty they all appeal to assumes that what it gives us in return for what we lose is equal to or better than the loss. Maybe this is also why I've come to prefer poems like "Easter 1916," which acknowledge something terrible in the beauty, to poems like "Sailing to Byzantium," which simply or uncritically celebrate the transformation of mutable experience into the immutable golden birds of art. Monumentalism feeds off the dead. It wants to replace the perishable flesh with imperishable stone; the bundle of accident that gets up for breakfast in the morning with the packed-in-salt immortal name. It wants us to feel that the transaction is a good one, that we've made a killing. And maybe we have.

I conclude by quoting from a poem called "Tourists" by the Israeli poet Yehudi Amichai. This is a poem that illustrates in style and subject an anti-monumentalist aesthetic, one that refuses the consolations and rationales we all fall back on when we talk about art, culture, or history in relation to the suffering of those on whom that art, that culture, that history, feeds. Here are the closing lines (that these lines are cast as prose, not "poetry," is itself an antimonumental gesture that underscores Amichai's allegiance to the evanescent but fundamental particulars of daily life):

Once I sat on the steps by a gate at David's Tower, I placed my two heavy baskets at my side. A group of tourists was standing around their guide and I became their target marker. "You see that man with the baskets? Just right of his head there's an arch from the Roman period. Just right of his head." "But he's moving, he's moving!" I said to myself: redemption will come only if their guide tells them, "You see that arch from the Roman period? It's not important: but next to it, left and down a bit, there sits a man who's bought fruit and vegetables for his family."

Because it is the nature of everything we love and value, of everything we are, to disappear, all artists are alchemists: we're all trying, all of us, no matter what our medium or stated principles may be, to transmute the base matter of mere life into the imperishable gold of art. Lately, though, that gold has come to feel like fool's gold, at least in its attempt to compensate us for the sorrows it expresses. At the same time, being fool's gold doesn't make it worthless.

If death is the mother of beauty, then I want the kind of beauty that acknowledges the insufficiency of beauty. I want the kind of art that admits it's giving us a song and dance when it transforms suffering into pleasure, pain into insight, life into clarifying images of life; the kind of art that recognizes there is no good substitute for the precious flesh. And that, recognizing this, apologizes for its own necessity.

Technique of Empathy:
Free Indirect Style

Let's say I want to write a narrative poem about an orthodox
Jew in the 1920s who also happens to be a much-sought-after
hit man for Murder Incorporated. Let's say his name is Manny
"the Moyel" Mandelbaum, and that because he's such a pious
Jew, he refuses to kill anyone on the Sabbath. Let's say the title
of the poem is "Guns and Mothers," and it opens like this:

Hester Street, 1923, a Friday evening, late fall, one hour
before sundown. Everywhere the smell of fish and chickpeas,
carts piled high with produce, street hawkers hawking beads,
garments, leather goods, candles. Steam rising through the
gratings and manhole covers up and down the neighborhood.
Next to the shul, the bakery. Next to the bakery, the deli, and
inside the deli, at his usual booth, wearing a suit to show he
was in business, and carrying a gun to show what business
he was in, Manny "the Moyel" was waiting for Sammy "the
Schnauz," the local bookie. "Thank God," he thought, glanc-
ing at the deli counter, "it's Mama's day off." He didn't want
her to see him getting rough with Sammy. She thought Manny
was in the funeral business. He hated lying to his mother, but
it would kill her if she knew the truth, and killing was a graver

sin than lying or working on the Sabbath. He was a good boy, a good son, he told himself, watching the door for Sammy, confident (if Sammy didn't show by sundown) he'd find him at the track on Saturday night.

This isn't bad, I think. Maybe a little stiff in its movement from full to limited omniscience, not quite as charged with Manny's subjectivity as I would like. Maybe if I cast the narrative entirely in limited third-person omniscience, it would acquire a bit more immediacy:

Wearing a suit to show he was in business, and carrying a gun to show what business he was in, Manny "the Moyel" entered Fleischman's Deli, looking for Sammy "the Schnauz," the local bookie. "Thank God," he told himself, "today is Mama's day off." He didn't want her to see him getting rough with Sammy. After all, she thought he was in the funeral business. That's what he told her he did for a living. See, he just hated lying to Mama. He shuddered to think what would happen if she ever knew what it was he really did. It would kill her. It would be worse than forgetting to call her on her birthday, worse than working on the Sabbath. He checked his watch. Only a half-hour before sundown. He scanned the joint, saw that Sammy wasn't in his usual booth, and left, thinking he'd find him at the track on Saturday night, if not at Lenny "the Loin"'s poker game on Sunday.

While this version carries a bit more feeling, it still seems more reportorial than I'd like ("he thought," "he shuddered"), the idiom still a little too removed from my character's subjectivity.

But there is a third option I can utilize, an option called free indirect style. Free indirect style is a subset of limited third person. While it isn't exclusive of full and limited omniscience, it can bring me closer to my character's perspective and sensibility without trapping me inside it. It's a style that can catch the tang of my speaker's voice without exactly quoting him:

Wearing a suit to show he was in business, and carrying a gun to show what business he was in, Manny "the Moyel" Mandelbaum slipped into Fleischman's Deli, looking for Sammy "the Schnauz," the local bookie. He glanced at the deli counter where his mother wasn't working, thank God. He didn't want she should see him getting rough with Sammy—not her son the undertaker. That's what he told her he did for a living. He hated lying to Mama, just hated it, and being an undertaker wasn't exactly a lie. God, if she ever knew what he really was, it would positively kill her. It would be worse than forgetting to call her on her birthday. And killing your mother, God forbid, was a graver sin than lying to her, please God it should never happen. He scanned the joint, checked his watch. Only a few minutes before sundown, and still no Sammy. Oh, he'd find the Schnauz, the little putz, sooner or later, at the track on Saturday night, if not at Lenny "the Loin"'s poker game on Sunday.

This version isn't as creaky as the other two. The narrative distance shifts smoothly from limited omnisicent to something close to but separate from first person, as we move from the first sentence to the ones that follow. "He didn't want her to see him getting rough with Sammy" becomes inflected with Manny's voice, his Yiddish/English syntax ("He didn't want she should see him . . ."). The elimination of the expository gestures, or speech tags—"he shuddered," "he thought," "he told himself"— transforms the scene from something reported to something dramatized, more immediately present. My character's idiom informs the narrative voice without becoming it. He appears not merely against the background of the narrator's imagination but also within his own. The narrative voice, in other words, is blended with the character's, and depending on how the story develops or where this scene falls in the overall arc of the piece, this blending of voices and points of view can be a source of empathy or irony or both. It can articulate a character's preverbal thoughts in an idiom the character himself would use if he could think them. It can let us see what he sees, feel what he feels, without confining what we see and feel only to his perspective and understanding. We see and feel beyond his horizon of vision even while we see and feel within it.

This inclusiveness and flexibility, this ability to move swiftly and without transition in and out of points of view and voices, is one of the great pleasures of this narrative mode. And the compression and speed it affords is especially suited to poetry, narrative or otherwise.

"The Mill," by E. A. Robinson, is a case in point:

The Miller's wife had waited long.
The tea was cold, the fire was dead.
And there might yet be nothing wrong
In how he went and what he said.
"There are no millers anymore"
Was all that she had heard him say.
And he had lingered at the door
So long that it seemed yesterday.

Sick with a fear that had no form
She knew that she was there at last.

And in the barn there was a warm
And mealy fragrance from the past.
What else was there would only seem
To say again what he had meant.
And what was hanging from a beam
Would not have heeded where she went.

And if she thought it followed her
She may have reasoned in the dark
That one way of the few there were
Would hide her and would leave no mark:
Black water smooth above the weir
Like starry velvet in the night
Though ruffled once would soon appear
The same as ever to the sight.

The wife's is the central point of view, yet the distance between the speaker's omniscient voice and hers is constantly shifting. The opening two lines are straight "objective" narration—
the voice seems entirely disentangled from the woman's—but
in the third line the two are merged. The phrasing catches her
attempting to convince herself that everything's OK. Had Robinson wanted to maintain an "objective" stance, he could have
simply flagged the wife's anxiety with something like "And she
was really really worried." Instead, he lets her inner voice, her
mental energy, contaminate his idiom; her speech suffuses his
without quite becoming it. And by the end of the stanza even
what at first appears "objective" seems retroactively tinted with
the dread and guilt she's trying not to feel. In light of everything the miller might have said but his wife didn't hear, even
the literal cold tea and dead fire of the second line foreshadow

her growing sense of having failed him; they seem retroactively expressive of her point of view.

The speaker returns to a more omniscient stance in the beginning of the second stanza, but that too quickly modulates back into free indirect speech, or something like it: "What else was there would only seem / to say again what he had meant. / And what was hanging from a beam / would not have heeded where she went." The indefinite pronoun *what* is the grammatical extension of her guilt, her averted gaze, her inability to face the consequences of her failure. And the switch to the conditional tense, which is then sustained for the remainder of the poem, expands our focus to include both the wife's perspective and the speaker's as he imagines what the water may look like to her in the moment before she plunges to her death. The conditional is the grammatical correlative of free indirect speech, the grammatical enactment of the empathy that wants to look out from within the body of the other even while acknowledging the other's separateness and mystery. Both free indirect speech and the conditional construction are thought experiments, driven by curiosity, on the one hand, and recognition, on the other, that our knowledge of other lives is guesswork, always incomplete, and thus our stories must be tentative, revisable— plausible at best, if never absolutely true.

"The Mill" is a plot-driven poem. It traces a double suicide. We follow the miller's wife from the house to the mill, where the miller has hanged himself, and then to the river where the wife will drown. It is remarkable in a poem describing such dramatic events that we get as much of her inner life as we do. On the other hand, "Donahue's Sister" by Thom Gunn is a poem in which after the first line nothing at all happens outside the character's consciousness. Which is not to say there is no plot,

but rather that the plot is entirely psychological, entirely driven
by a single point of view:

> She comes level with him at
> the head of the stairs
> with a slight, arrogant smile
> and an inward look, muttering
> some injunction to her private world.
> Drunk for four days now.
>
> He's unable to get through.
> She's not there to get through to.
> When he does get through,
> next week, it will all sound
> exaggerated. She will apologize as if
> all too humanly she has caused him
> a minute inconvenience.
>
> That sudden tirade last night,
> such conviction and logic
> —had she always hated him or
> was it the zombie speaking?
>
> Scotch for breakfast,
> beer all morning.
> Fuelling her private world, in which
> she builds her case against the public.
> Catching at ends of phrases
> in themselves meaningless,
> as if to demonstrate how well
> she keeps abreast.

A zombie,
inaccessible and sodden replacement.

He glances at her, her
body stands light and meatless,
and estimates how high he would have
to lift it to launch it
into a perfect trajectory over
the narrow dark staircase
so that it would land on its head
on the apartment-house mosaic of the hallway
and its skull would break in two
—an eggshell full of alcohol—
leaving, at last, his sister
lying like the garbage by the front door
in a pool of Scotch and beer,
understandably, this time, inaccessible.

Everything we see is through the brother's eyes. The narrative voice is entirely submerged within Donohue's internal speech. His frustration and impotence infuse everything: they govern the poem's many temporal shifts (present to past to present to future to more recent past, back to present); shape the imagery and idiom ("had she always hated him or / was it the zombie speaking?"); and, most remarkably, determine both the syntax and its relation to the line. The opening stanza, for instance, consists of a long compound sentence and a one-line adjectival fragment. The long sentence sets up the expectation that some dramatic confrontation is about to happen ("She comes level with him at / the head of the stairs . . ."). But what begins as a promise of decisive action ends with a fragmentary phrase, a phrase without an active verb, the syntactical effect of being blocked and helpless, unable to effect any kind of change at all. The two short sentences that follow this fragment coincide with the short lines and end with prepositions, prepositions which strain awkwardly and painfully after some release or breakthrough which again does not occur ("He's unable to get through. / She's not there to get through to. / When he does get through . . ."). It's the purpose of a preposition to move us forward or place a subject in relation to an object, to relate the two. But here there is no relation, and the prepositions that gum up the end lines and rhyme so clumsily impede our movement and thus reinforce the brother's entrapment. Even the long conditional sentence that concludes the poem with a fantasy of escape through violence ironically increases the feeling of impotence, since it occurs in imagination only, in wish but not in fact.

The poem illustrates free indirect speech at its most expressive. It brings into play a medley of voices—we hear the narrative voice inflected with the brother's voice that is, in turn, inflected with the sister's as he recalls her drunken rants and self-justifications: "She will apologize / as if all too humanly she has caused him / a minute inconvenience." The complex blending of idioms reflects how deeply and hopelessly entangled these two lives have become; it is itself an image of a paralyzing codependency.

At its most powerful, free indirect speech can be an instrument of moral exploration. Its advantage over direct speech is that it's capable of going beyond the conscious verbalization that constrains dramatic monologue; it can articulate the half-thought or the unthought, the confused or unconfronted. It can avoid the coolness of indirect third-person speech while retaining a clarifying distance, a wider horizon of vision. It can evoke even while it analyzes.

Here's another poem by Gunn that uses free indirect speech in a more restrained way yet illustrates how the technique can reverberate through a poem even when it isn't being explicitly used. It's called "Slow Waker":

I look at the nephew,
eighteen, across the breakfast.
He had to be called and called.
He smiles, but without
conviction. He will not
have tea, oh OK,
if it's no trouble,
he will have tea.

His adult face is brand-new.
Once the newness
clears up and it has got
an expression or two
besides bewilderment
he could be a handsome
devil. He could be
a carpenter, a poet, it's
all possible . . .
impossible. The future
is not a word in his mouth.

That, for him, is the trouble:
he lay in bed caught deep
in the mire between
sleep and awake, neither
alert nor resting,

between the flow of night
ceaselessly braiding itself,
and the gravelly beach
that our soles have thickened on.
Nobody has ever told him
he is good-looking,
just that his feet smell.

He paces through alien London
all day. Everything
is important and unimportant.
He feeds only by osmosis.
He stares at the glint
and blunt thrust of traffic. He
wants to withdraw.

He wants to withdraw into
a small place, like
the cupboard under the stairs
where the vacuum cleaner is kept,
so he can wait, and doze,
and get in nobody's way.

The speaker here is not a "nonpersonal" narrator as in all the other examples but a participant in the scene itself, sitting across from his nephew at the breakfast table. Free indirect speech appears as vocal mimicry at first, a gesture more affectionately ironic than empathic. But the contradictory shape of it—"He will not . . . oh OK . . . he will . . ."—provides the syntactical template for the speaker's evocation in his own voice of the nephew's indeterminate identity, his in-between condition, neither boy nor man, in which everything is possible and impossible, important and unimportant, neither fully awake nor sleeping, neither resting nor alert, between the flow of night and the gravelly beach. Unlike in "Donohue's Sister," where the speaker speaks from within the brother's voice and point of view, here the speaker remains outside the boy's perspective, looking in. The distance, though, is qualified by the repeated conditionals, the negative constructions, and the antitheses, all of which bear the stamp of that initial bit of mimicked speech ("He will not . . . oh OK . . . he will . . .").

Even though technically free indirect speech appears only in those opening lines, the empathic spirit of it permeates everything that follows. In the fourth stanza, we get three short simple sentences all in the narrator's voice, but each one moving closer to the boy's perspective: "He feeds only by osmosis. / He stares at the glint / and blunt thrust of traffic. He / wants to withdraw." The first sentence takes us back to the nephew at the breakfast table, wanting and not wanting tea. Like *future*, *osmosis* is probably not a word the boy would use even while it's a completely credible inference drawn from everything preceding it. The next sentence shifts from abstraction to imagery and thus in a way moves closer to the boy's emotional situation, his confusion and vulnerability. Or better yet, think of the images as an imaginative translation of the boy's inchoate perspective into the speaker's empathic understanding of it: "He stares at the glint / and blunt thrust of traffic." If there's any mimicry here it's in the rhythm, the alternation of clustering heavy and light stresses ("glint / and blunt thrust") that suggest both the sensory impact of the world on the boy's overwhelmed and foggy sensibility and his newly emerged yet diffuse sexuality. And there's also mimicry, or something like mimicry, in the breaking of the next sentence across two lines: the repetition of the pronoun *he* and its conspicuous placement at the end of the stanza's penultimate line call attention to the boy's self-conscious isolation, the feeling of which, intensified by the repetition in the next line ("he wants to withdraw"), governs the more homely language of withdrawal into the closet under the stairs where the vacuum cleaner is kept, a metonymic figure of regression drawn from the boy's literal circumstances. In effect, we come full circle: back to the house where we started, to details which are in a way the objective correlatives of the boy's voice, a kind of imagistic free indirect speech. The language returns to the mundane and banal, so close to the boy's perspective, from the speaker's more elaborate "poetic" language earlier of the flow of night and gravelly beach, a poetic idiom far removed from the boy's voice and thus more expressive of the speaker's empathic understanding of the nephew than of the nephew's understanding of himself.

Like "Slow Waker," "A Fantasy" by Louise Glück deploys a single instance of free indirect style, and yet that instance, as in "Slow Waker," provides the pivot on which the narrator turns empathically from an outside perspective on widows and orphans to a perspective within a particular woman whose anguish and helplessness produce (in the midst of the social conventions of mourning) an unconventional and unattainable fantasy in the closing lines:

I'll tell you something, every day
people are dying. And that's just the beginning.
Every day in funeral homes, new widows are born,
new orphans. They sit with their hands folded,
trying to decide about this new life.

Then they're in the cemetery, some of them
for the first time. They're frightened of crying,
sometimes of not crying. Someone leans over,
tells them what to do next, which might mean
saying a few words, sometimes
throwing dirt in the open grave.

And after that, everyone goes back to the house,
which is suddenly full of visitors.
The widow sits on the couch, very stately,
so people line up to approach her,
sometimes take her hand, sometimes embrace her.
She finds something to say to everybody,
Thanks them, thanks them for coming.

In her heart, she wants them to go away.
She wants to be back in the cemetery,
back in the sick room, the hospital. She knows
it isn't possible. But it's her only hope,
the wish to move backwards, and just a little,
not so far as the marriage, the first kiss.

The poem turns dramatically after the one line of free indirect speech, "Thanks them, thanks them for coming." There has been an implicit lyric urgency throughout the poem, an urgency signaled by those opening lines, "I'll tell you something . . . / people are dying." Is the speaker speaking to a specific someone, or is she talking to us? Have we entered the poem in the middle of an animated conversation, if not an argument? And while no one person's point of view (besides the narrator's) governs the opening two stanzas, once we enter the house of this specific widow her perspective subtly emerges from the adverbs *suddenly* and *stately*, but it's only after her voice, her idiom, inflects the narrator's that we enter her subjectivity: "In her heart, she wants them to go away." It's as if Glück first had to let the widow's vocal show of well-mannered earnestness resonate within the voice of her narrator before she'd let the narrator enter the widow's psyche, where we see and feel the desperation ("it's her only hope") hidden behind the "stately" mask. While up to this point we see mostly the face of customary mourning that the newborn widows and orphans are struggling to learn, in the closing lines we go beyond convention into an anguished fantasy of turning back the clock. The fantasy is an odd one, modest in its way (is it so much to ask to go back in time just a little, to the immediate past of the sick room and the hospital?), but it also seems a little creepy. Maybe the marriage wasn't so great to begin with, or maybe the suffering and caretaking have made the presickness phase of the marriage seem unimaginably remote. Either way, we feel her devastating realization of the inexorability of loss, the irreversibility of time, all of which, I think, springs subtly yet powerfully from that little bit of free indirect speech at the end of the previous stanza. The widow's voice, her speech, is the gateway to her heart.

In some quarters of the literary world, there is a great distrust—if not dislike—of narrative. The arguments against narrative go back at least a hundred years. While they have taken many forms, serving different purposes, the one assumption shared by all of them, early and late, modern and postmodern, is that formal devices falsify reality. Narrative order is a myth that bears no relation to experience as it is actually lived. The world is unknowable, other lives are inaccessible, and omniscience and narrative pattern are at best escapist fantasies, at worst tools of political and psychological manipulation. While the narrative device of free indirect speech has been around for centuries, it is only in the nineteenth and twentieth centuries that it becomes more than verbal mimicry. In the last century especially, novelists have used it to explore the workings of consciousness in ever more refined and sensitive ways (e.g., Roy Pascal in his *The Dual Voice*). Insofar as it enables narrative to move deeper into subjectivity, free indirect speech is symptomatic of a loss of faith in an objective world external to the self, a world that's shared with others. The narrators we trust or recognize as one of us don't speak with godlike authority about the inner lives of other people. They tend to keep their opinions to themselves. They keep close to the grain of their character's point of view. They don't moralize, except perhaps implicitly in and through their choice of subject matter, what events and incidents they bring into relation, and in how their plots are structured. They limit their language and perceptions, as much as possible, to the language and perceptions of their characters.

And yet as Leo Spitzer points out, mimicry itself implies a mimic as well as a person, someone who is morally engaged with the people in his fictional world, with people he believes it's in our interest as curious and vulnerable fellow human beings to pay attention to in precisely the ways that his imagination says we should. Free indirect speech presupposes the value of empathic understanding. It does assume we live in a world of competing points of view and interests, a world intractable to any easy understanding or judgment, but a world we nonetheless must struggle to make sense of as best we can. The refusal to abandon the third-person pronoun bespeaks a commitment to the ideal of shared understanding even while the limited omniscience reminds us how difficult it is to know each other or ourselves. Free indirect speech is the fictional equivalent of a thought experiment, an imaginative hunch or informed guess. It asks us to consider becoming someone else, not as an as-is proposition but as an as-if or what-if exercise. It is the fictional spirit of the subjunctive mood.

In the last thirty years or so, many poets have turned back to narrative along with other modes of writing that had fallen out of favor in the modern and postmodern periods. This move has been motivated partly by a desire to reinvigorate poetry by enlarging its expressive repertoire, repossessing territory it had ceded to prose genres over the last few hundred years. In the best examples, in C. K. Williams, Robert Pinsky, James McMichael, Tom Sleigh, Spenser Reece, and many others I could name, the return to narrative is informed by all the arguments against narrative. It shares postmodern anxieties about representation, the limits of language, and the many ways linguistic conventions of any kind can exclude, distort, or oversimplify. It is alert, as well, to the dangers of mere anecdote and the dullness of plodding linearity. What perhaps distinguishes these poets from their more postmodern counterparts is a belief in storytelling as a mode of thinking about other lives, an imaginative thinking, however qualified or hedged by skepticism, that's embedded in the psychosocial circumstances within which people live.

As I have tried to show, free indirect speech is driven by that tentative or postmodern uncertainty, even while it preserves a vestige of the omniscience it no longer trusts. In a way, free indirect speech, at its most profound, represents an interplay of the old and new—between the civil dream of imagining past differences of race, gender, and class to a shared understanding of ourselves and one another, and an acute awareness of just how intractable those differences can be. In the hands of our best poets and storytellers, it establishes a superimposition in which characters appear both against the background of the narrator's imagination and also within their own. It enables us to hear both the narrator struggling to get the characters' stories right and the stories the characters themselves are struggling to tell. Free indirect speech is vocalized empathy, a technique suited to and required by a pluralistic world.

Thirteen Ways of Looking at Decorum

1

Oh I can picture all manner of yawns, groans, teeth gnashing, and rolling of eyes at the very mention of the word *decorum*, never mind my sense of it as an animating indispensable principle of all good poems and stories. I realize that to talk about decorum in this day and age of gender bending, cultural relativism, and ever-accelerating social change and technological innovation is to risk a kind of fusty, uptight moralism. Like Marxism, in America anyway at this particular moment, it's a tough sell for sure, a little like arguing that Elizabethan collars, farthingales, frock coats, and iron chastity belts are hot and trending. Along with the romantics, most of us associate decorum, if we think of it at all, with repressive neoclassical rules of taste, that is, with overrefined, anachronistic vestiges of a more stable and hierarchical culture. I mean, consider its definition and etymology: "noun, meaning appropriate behavior. Before 1568, borrowing of Latin *decorum*, that which is proper or seemly, noun use of the neuter singular of the adjective decorus, related to decere, meaning, be proper; see DECENT." As if this weren't bad enough, out of its Latin root by way of French we can thank *decorum* for words like *décor* and *decoration*.

When we think of the literary virtues (*virtues*, another boring word) we look for in our favorite stories and poems, decorum, decor, ornament, good behavior, decency aren't exactly in anybody's top-ten list of desired qualities ("This is a really well behaved poem!" "Wow, this poem is so, so very decent!"). The very notion of decorum runs counter to prevailing taste; it embodies everything we hate in art: normality, conventionality, conformity, niceness—it is, in short, the opposite of self-expression, surprise, excitement, the dangerous and thrilling, the disjunctive, the fresh and new.

If my subject here were pattern, not decorum, I'd have an easier time of it. We talk incessantly, as we should, about sonic and semantic pattern, about the inescapable role of pattern in our experience of art, knowing that without the expectation of something repeated, there's no chance of surprise and variation. We're told by neuroscience and evolutionary biology that our avidity for pattern is a human universal—that our minds are pattern junkies. "Pattern recognition," Brian Boyd argues in *On the Origin of Stories*, "lets us distinguish animate from inanimate, human from nonhuman, this individual from all others, this attitude or expression from another. The capacity to identify not only individuals but higher order tendencies in behavior, personality and powers allows for invaluably precise prediction." Negative connotations haven't stuck to the word or idea of pattern, even though it has a similar etymological history to decorum's—deriving from the medieval Latin word *patronus*, or patron. The transfer of sense from *patron* to repeatable form or example developed from the idea of a patron, a boss, a rich guy, the personification of masculinity, as a model to be imitated; only in the late-sixteenth century was the meaning of pattern extended to decorative or artistic design, for things like china, carpets, and wallpaper, not exactly what we think about when we think about great art. Why pattern isn't tainted by its history while decorum continues to be is not a question I can answer, at least not here. What I aim to do is disentangle decorum from its association with predetermined rules of behavior fit only for a drawing room, and show how it's an openended form of thinking and feeling more closely aligned with imagination than with any repressive moral code or stifling moralism.

$$2$$

Let's assume for the sake of argument that hunger for information is a universal appetite, a design feature of all minds, human and nonhuman alike. Ability to predict the future based on the regularities we see around us has been a key element in our survival as a species. From past experience, I know that that disturbance in the tall grass over there may be a lion. That loud noise beyond that hill up ahead may be a rival tribe. I'm more likely to mistake a garden hose for a snake than a snake for a garden hose. These lightning-fast inferences arise from encounters with past situations, some reaching back to our primate past. But no two situations are ever the same, so the application of past experience to present circumstance (otherwise known as memory) has to be made flexibly and loosely. But here's a complication. If pattern is, so to speak, the PATRON saint of information, isn't it also true that when a pattern becomes too expected, too predictable, it ceases to inform? It grows invisible through habituation. It turns into white noise, a uniform chaos insofar as it no longer offers any knowledge for the mind to extract, and so the mind just stops attending,

which, from a survival standpoint, can be potentially dangerous. Think in this respect of method-driven forms of poetry,
poetry either embodying a monolithic concept or idea, which it
repeats without variation ad infinitum, or that refuses any and
all pattern in favor of unvarying disjunction. Or at the opposite end of the poetry spectrum, think of metrical verse that's
merely metrical, merely a zombielike march of iambs with no
rhythmical variation, no sonic responsiveness to changes in
tone or feeling. The totally patterned and the total absence of
pattern amount to the same thing. The mind shuts off in the
presence of both. So if the detection of information in literature arises from an interplay of pattern and variation, or from
new patterns emerging from old patterns, then maybe we can
think of decorum as the mental agility and emotional alertness
that does the detecting.

Akin to Shelley's definition of imagination as a kind of
muscle of attention, decorum can be thought of as a keen and
sensitive awareness that is ever open to and on the lookout for
new patterns, while testing old ones against an ever-changing
world. "Frogs react," Boyd tells us, "with an automatic flick of
the tongue to small objects flying across their field of vision.
That makes them swifter than you or I at catching insects, but
they cannot respond to new kinds of patterns." Decorum is
that capacity for responsiveness, that mental and emotional
poise that knows that each encounter, each moment of experience, on the page or in the world, may or may not conform to
expectation—decorum in this respect requires a readiness to
improvise. It requires both a knowledge of pattern and regular-
ity and an existential improvisatory openness to the unfore-
seen, the unanticipated, in order to make the richest, most
inclusive inferences from the situation at hand.

3

The little-known seventeenth-century colonial poet Philip Pain drowned in a shipwreck off the coast of New England when he was twenty-two years old. Shortly before his death, he wrote the following prophetic poem, a short, meditative epigram on the difference between the general idea of the inevitability of death and the realization that you yourself will someday die:

> Scarce do I pass a day but that I hear
> Someone or other's dead, and to my ear
> Methinks it is no news. But Oh! Did I
> Think deeply on it, what it is to die,
> My pulses all would beat, I should not be
> Drowned in this deluge of security.

After the first sentence, the poem turns from dispassionate knowing, something the self registers only with the ear, to knowing with the entire body—knowledge carried from ear and mind to heart to the speaker's very nerve ends. The lack of emotional engagement that comes with knowing something merely with the mind or ear, mind's metonymic figure, is nicely suggested by the blandly regular cadence of lines 1 and 2. The sentence glides as easily from first couplet to second couplet as the news of death passes into and out of the ear that hears it. The second sentence signals the turn to a fuller response not just by "But," the adversative conjunction, but also by the heavily stressed syllables of the last two feet of line 3 and the relatively unstable line break after "I"—the rhythm weighted down with stress gets weightier and slower from the heavily stressed first foot of line four ("Think deeply . . .") and by where the pause falls in the line, in the middle of the third foot, which alters by muting the iambic cadence even further. Compare that pause with the pause in line 2, which falls after, not in the middle of, the third foot.

When the metrical unit and the grammatical clause coincide, there's little or no disruption, the cadence is not disturbed to the degree it is when the grammar and meter fall out of phase as they do here. The shift in focus from death as general phenomenon to death as personal (if imagined) experience is further reinforced by the rhyme of "I" and "die" and the comma after "die," which stops us from sailing past the word (as we sail past "ear" and "hear" in the first couplet). We can't help but feel viscerally to our very core what it means to die.

One last point. The conditional verb tense of the final sentence suggests that the very thought experiment the poem is conducting would be too terrifying, too overwhelming, to carry out. We're given instead a thought experiment of a thought experiment, an imagining of what would happen if the speaker were to imagine what no one can really imagine. And then there's a last turn in the final line, where what the poet's drowning in is not a deluge of death itself but a deluge of security, the false security of not thinking deeply, which he implies is like a death in life, just as to imagine thinking deeply about death is to arouse the body to an almost unbearable terrifying vitality. The powerful trochaic substitution in the first foot is like a terrible awakening. And the way the *d* of "deluge" pulls after it the *d* of "drowned" quickens the fall into the word *security*, which comprises the last two feet of the poem—a paradox in and of itself, inasmuch as these feet as iambs aren't terribly emphatic, stable, or secure—and yet they coincide with a synonym for "stability."

What enables Pain to dramatize the difference between knowing and realizing, the way he makes the language embody the realization it performs, is a measure of what I would like to call poetic decorum—decorum as sensitive and tactful management of sound and sense to make the fullest, most inclusive rendering of an experience. The poem derives from a truism: all living things die. "Methinks it is no news." But what distinguishes the poem from the truism, what *is* news that stays news, is the extent to which the poem discovers the truth of the truism, as Yvor Winters once remarked in relation to the plain style, in and through the particulars of experience.

4

I was first introduced to *decorum* as a literary term in the early 1970s at Brandeis University, on the first day of my undergraduate poetry workshop with Galway Kinnell. Kinnell invoked decorum negatively while explaining why he wouldn't allow anyone in the class to write in rhyme and meter. The forms and styles we write in, he told us, are inescapably tied to and expressions of our historical moment. The metrical poetry of sixteenth- and seventeenth-century poets, and their concept of genres and levels of style corresponding to those genres, reflected a more traditional, more stable society (well, tell that to Anne Boleyn, King Charles, or John Tyndall). Theirs was a universe whose core myth was the great chain of being— every form of life and every individual and every human faculty within each individual existed in predetermined, God-appointed mutually reinforcing hierarchies—from peasant to yeoman, nobility to king in the body politic, from animal appetite to will to reason in the self, and from plain style for low subjects, middle or sweet style for pastoral and romance, to high style for epic in the practice of the literary arts.

Our twenty-first-century universe, on the other hand, has no such foundational myth and thus no such rigidly determined sense of what kinds of language, forms, and styles are appropriate for what kinds of occasion, character, and action. According to Kinnell, the classical idea of decorum ratified the forms of Elizabethan poetry. But since our world possesses no mutually agreed-upon concept of what should go with what, decorum as an organizing concept is no longer relevant. It is as antiquated as the forms it once legitimized. "Our world," Kinnell movingly said—and now I'm quoting from what I'd written down that day in class—"is not so neat and small. We don't believe we're at the center of anything. We live on a dying inconspicuous planet in a corner of an infinitely expanding universe. Our social order, driven by money and power, is fragmented, heterogeneous, mobile, and vast. The old forms and canons of taste no longer apply."

Kinnell's deterministic vision of the Elizabethan world and its literary practices and of literary practice in general seems now, if it didn't back in the 1970s, a bit reductive. It's a narrative that for me personally as well as for many poets of my generation and the generation after mine became a kind of gospel, an ironclad orthodoxy, which self-servingly justified historical ignorance, even though that's not at all what Kinnell intended. Because our world had changed so dramatically from the older, whiter, more patriarchal world of earlier poets, we no longer needed to learn about poetry written before the present moment. Those older poets were, as we used to say, no longer relevant. But what even a cursory survey of English poetry before the nineteenth century will show is that there's nothing inherently old-fashioned or new-fashioned about the forms one writes in. And while the concept of decorum was important in the sixteenth and seventeenth centuries, it had not, as it had to some degree by the eighteenth century, ossified into a rigid set of rules and tenets, into what Wordsworth would contemptuously refer to as false refinement and poetic diction. Yes, language was adjusted to occasion: grand themes and subjects were treated in an elevated epic style, while humble and trivial subjects were treated in a low and/or vulgar manner— see George Gascoigne's "Woodmanship" or John Skelton's "The Tunnyng of Elynour Rummyng"—but the rules weren't hard and fast; many of these poets often violate the very conventions they invoke. Decorum is applied much more flexibly and strangely than Kinnell's depiction would imply.

5

J. V. Cunningham, who taught at Brandeis at the same time as Kinnell, provided an alternative perspective on poetic conventions like rhyme and meter. In Cunningham's view, the forms we write in are, of course, informed by history, but their usefulness as technologies of feeling aren't confined entirely to the times that spawned them. Cunningham was famous for writing epigrams, a genre of verse that originated in ancient Greece in the Hellenistic period. Though traditionally associated with short, witty, often satirical sendups of human foibles, the epigram has actually served a wide array of subjects over the centuries, everything from the smutty to the sacred. It became quite popular among seventeenth-century English poets, Ben Jonson especially. No one in the twentieth or twenty-first century has turned to the epigram quite as often or with as much skill as Cunningham. Here's one of his that reconceives in a new and very modern light the commonplace that time heals old wounds:

Deep summer, and time pauses. Sorrow wastes
To a new sorrow. While time heals time hastes.

In the space of a single iambic pentameter couplet, we find three different kinds of sentences. The first is a compound sentence whose first half is a fragment. The fragmentary appearance coincides with and reinforces the feeling of time standing still. The next two sentences, however, undercut that deep summer feeling of temporal stasis—the second sentence, broken across the two lines, invites the possibility that sorrow is about to waste away into something different, joy or relief from pain, a possibility which the continuation of the sentence both intensifies and deflates: the pyrrhic-spondee combination in the first two feet of line two quickens the rhythm and then abruptly stops it at "new sorrow." Out of the assertion that sorrow leads to sorrow even in the deepest part of summer, when time seems to be standing still, comes the grim joke of the final sentence, which essentially restates the second sentence by reversing the old saw "Time heals all wounds."

What amazes me about this poem is the management of sound and rhythm, how the sensation of time pausing along with the realization that time never pauses is enacted by the interplay of grammar and metrical feet. Notice how every pause in the poem falls in the middle of a foot, so that even while the grammar comes to a stop, the meter pulls us forward. The one time a pause falls more stably after a foot is in the middle of final sentence ("While time heals") where there's a natural pause between dependent clause and main clause, even if there is no comma, but this slight pause before the main clause only intensifies the reversal of good news implicit in "heals" to the bad news implicit in "hastes." One last observation: the last four monosyllabic words of the poem are all heavily stressed, but the stresses create antithetical effects—the alliteration that connects "heals" to "hastes" only highlights a semantic and sonic difference, the long *l* of "heals" giving way to the quick sharp sibilance of "hastes," enacting on the level of sound the way time hastens even when we think it doesn't.

The poem is alert to its emotion and thought on every level, shifting in sound and speed as the feeling shifts. There's nothing antiquated or fussy about it. Nothing in my view closed or formal in its handling of form. It seems alive to its own occasion and necessity. That is, it's decorous in a way that is both timely and (relatively speaking) timeless.

6

I still think Kinnell in some respects was right. History does shape or influence, for good or ill, our sense of decorum, our determination of how much is too much or too little, even if the way it does so isn't quite as straightforward as Kinnell suggested. Take Milton, for example. *Paradise Lost* treats a grand theme in a dignified and noble style. But Milton sweepingly dismisses rhyme in epic poetry as "the invention of a barbarous age." In the course of the poem, too, he mixes the domestic or romantic and sometimes shockingly intimate with the heroic, as when Adam asks the blushing Gabriel if angels have sex. That is, when he wanted to, when it suited his interests, he abandoned or reworked inherited conventions and received ideas, or brought together forms and styles that the classical idea of decorum would have urged the poets of his time to keep apart. In one breath Milton can describe decorum as the grand masterpiece to be observed at all times in any work of art, and in the next he can overturn convention in ways, I should add, that don't always improve the poems.

The following two poems are a case in point. They're both Petrarchan sonnets that are also letter poems, verse epistles that are also invitation poems that, in turn, are also friendship poems, poems that implicitly define what a friendship is or should be. And to all of this Milton adds something like the elevated style of epic poetry:

Cyrick, whose grandsire on the royal bench
Of British Themis, with no mean applause,
Pronounced, and in his volumes taught, our laws,
Which others at their bar so often wrench,
Today deep thoughts resolve with me to drench
In mirth that after no repenting draws;
Let Euclid rest, and Archimedes pause,
And what the Swede intend, and what the French.
To measure life learn thou betimes, and know
Toward solid good what leads the nearest way;
For other things mild Heaven a time ordains,
And disapproves that care, though wise in show,
That with superfluous burden loads the day,
And, when God sends a cheerful hour, refrains.

Lawrence, of virtuous father virtuous son,
Now that the fields are dank, and ways are mire,
Where shall we sometimes meet, and by the fire
Help waste a sullen day; what may be won
From the hard season gaining? Time will run
On smoother, till Favonius re-inspire
The frozen earth, and clothe in fresh attire
The lily and rose, that neither sow'd nor spun.
What neat repast shall feast us, light and choice,

Of Attic taste, with wine, whence we may rise
To hear the lute well touch'd, or artful voice
Warble immortal notes and Tuscan air?
He who of those delights can judge, and spare
To interpose them oft, is not unwise.

Is it just our distance in time that makes both poems, despite
the fantastic management of form and syntax and overall elegance, seem like an inadvertently comical mismatch of style
and content? In both poems, Milton, channeling Horace, urges
his young friends to kick back and take it easy. In "Cyrick," the
poet invites his friend, a lawyer, to take a break from the legal
bar and at a local bar "drench in mirth" "a cheerful hour." In
"Lawrence," he advises a young farmer, during the winter, when
no farming can be done, to sit by the fire, eat, drink wine, and
listen to someone play the lute and sing. But the Latinate syntax
of both poems, with its long periods and inverted phrasing, and
the overall formality of tone contain more Virgil than Horace;
what's missing are Horace's urbanity, humor, and warmth, his
plainer diction, which make Horace's odes and epistles composed fifteen hundred years before Milton seem so much closer
to the twenty-first century than Milton does, in these sonnets
anyway. It's like Milton has appeared for an evening of beer
pong dressed up as Aeneas. This is a style, in other words, more
appropriate for justifying God's ways to man than for chillin' at
the crib with a couple of homies.

7

One of Ben Jonson's drinking haunts was the Old Devil Tavern.
He and his friends were such regulars that the owner set aside
a special room for them called the Apollo, for which Jonson

wrote, in Latin, the house rules, the Leges Convivales. Many of these rules are borrowed from invitation/verse epistles and epigrams by Horace and Martial, and according to Jonson scholars they are written in the same flexible and idiomatic Latin those classical poets employed. As you'll see these house rules could easily apply to, if not describe, our residencies and writing conferences. Here's a translation of some of them by Jonson scholar Wesley Trimpi:

> Let no one who will pay for nothing come, unless he be a guest of someone who has been officially invited. Let the insipid, melancholy and frowzy fool stay away; let the learned, the urbane, the gay and the honest be admitted. . . . Let the dishes be prepared with refined taste rather than expense. . . . The wine must be drawn from fountains which admit no dilute mixture, or else the host must be punished. . . . Let no guest talk too much or be silent, and let no one who is full of food and drink discourse on serious or sacred matters. . . . It is allowed that our private mysteries be celebrated with laughter, dances, choruses, songs, jokes, and all the festivities of the Graces. All jokes must be without gall, and no flat poems may be recited; let none be compelled to write verses. There must be no clamor of argument, but let there be a free corner for the sighs and disputes of lovers. No one shall be permitted to fight with great goblets in the manner of the Lapithians, to break glassware, to knock out windows, or rip apart furniture. Let him be let out who lets out to the world what we do or say, for the liquor must make no one a culprit. Let the fire always be burning.

These rules and their classical antecedents are what Jonson drew from in his great poem "Inviting a Friend to Supper"— written some thirty or forty years earlier than Milton's sonnets:

Tonight, grave sir, both my poor house, and I
Do equally desire your company;
Not that we think us worthy such a guest,
But that your worth will dignify our feast
With those that come, whose grace may make that seem
Something, which else could hope for no esteem.
It is the fair acceptance, sir, creates
The entertainment perfect, not the cates.
Yet shall you have, to rectify your palate,
An olive, capers, or some better salad
Ushering the mutton; with a short-legged hen,
If we can get her, full of eggs, and then
Lemons, and wine for sauce; to these a cony
Is not to be despaired of, for our money;
And, though fowl now be scarce, yet there are clerks,
The sky not falling, think we may have larks.
I'll tell you of more, and lie, so you will come:
Of partridge, pheasant, woodcock, of which some
May yet be there, and godwit, if we can;
Knat, rail, and ruff too. Howsoe'er, my man
Shall read a piece of Virgil, Tacitus,
Livy, or of some better book to us,
Of which we'll speak our minds, amidst our meat;
And I'll profess no verses to repeat.
To this, if ought appear which I not know of,
That will the pastry, not my paper, show of.
Digestive cheese and fruit there sure will be;
But that which most doth take my Muse and me,
Is a pure cup of rich Canary wine,
Which is the Mermaid's now, but shall be mine;
Of which had Horace, or Anacreon tasted,
Their lives, as so their lines, till now had lasted.

Tobacco, nectar, or the Thespian spring,
Are all but Luther's beer to this I sing.
Of this we will sup free, but moderately,
And we will have no Pooley, or Parrot by,
Nor shall our cups make any guilty men;
But, at our parting we will be as when
We innocently met. No simple word
That shall be uttered at our mirthful board,
Shall make us sad next morning or affright
The liberty that we'll enjoy tonight.

The poem performs the entertainment that it promises. Liberty with moderation, intimacy with restraint, impulse and control, the acknowledgment of social norms and the freedom to suspend them within limits when the moment requires, all this is embodied by the ongoing delicate push-pull of syntax and line, syntax and couplet. The rhymes fall almost by accident, and the phrases flexibly contract and lengthen, shifting the pauses within or between the lines so as to build anticipation and surprise, the way a good comic does, while orchestrating our attention from moments of playful exaggeration ("I'll tell you of more, and lie, so you will come: / Of partridge, pheasant, woodcock of which some / May yet be there") to witty self-deprecation ("we'll speak our minds, amidst our meat; / And I'll profess no verses to repeat") to passages of intimate earnestness ("Of this we will sup free, but moderately"). Like a good dinner host, Jonson manages the form with a noticeably unnoticeable facility, shaping the sentences and breaking them across the lines so as to vocalize these tonal nuances. In a way you can see the informal, casual-seeming sentences wandering in and out of the couplets, sometimes in phase with them and sometimes not, as the syntactical expression of the liberty the friends will enjoy, and you can likewise see the formal elements of meter and couplet as expressions of moderation, the need for flexible limits.

Sometimes the balance of power in the poem tilts more toward freedom, sometimes more toward restraint. But at every point in the poem you feel the pressure of both. Moderation and liberty reinforce each other—together they promote by enacting a kind of Aristotelian inclusiveness, the kind of decorum that's both literary and social—which inheres in a flexible alertness that enables the widest possible range of pleasure (food, drink, books, intimacy, jokes, trust, tolerance of imperfections, etc.) and the narrowest possible range of pain (no hangover, no insults or excesses born of too much wine). An evening with friends will be more enjoyable the more fully accessible we are to one another. To drink or eat excessively would be to pursue the pleasure of food and alcohol to the exclusion of conversation, or risk becoming so uninhibited you say something stupid or dangerous that you'll regret the following morning. To talk only about books without eating or drinking would be boring at best, and eventually hunger and thirst would distract attention from the intellectual pleasures to be had. To dominate a conversation or to insist on showing off, foisting your own private *Iliad* upon your friends or nattering on all night about your own concerns and obsessions, would cut you off from the pleasure of other minds. Moderation in this Aristotelian sense is in the interests of liberty. It is to make those choices that permit the greatest number of subsequent choices, so as to keep us open to the greatest range of experiential possibility. Compare this poem with Milton's and ask yourself: which invitation would I rather accept?

8

Social norms, like literary norms, are ever changing but ever present. They develop in response to changing circumstances, to mutable environments that they, for a while, enable us to navigate until sooner or later they outlive their usefulness, to be abandoned, as Philip Larkin says in "High Windows," like an outdated combine harvester, in favor of new or emergent ways of living and writing. What appears as outrageous brutality to a twenty-first-century Western sensibility might have seemed to a sensibility of an earlier age like a model of decency. When a violent mob in Sodom demands that Lot give up the angelic strangers he is hosting, and he instead pushes his young daughter out the door so she's the one who's raped and killed, I'm sure the ancient Hebrews saw him as a paragon of faith and hospitality, a model of piety, though few of us now would share that judgment. If my wife and I are eating at a restaurant and the food is so to-die-for delicious that I offer the chef as a token of appreciation my wife or daughter as a bedmate, no one I know would nominate me for a Father- or Husband-of-the-Year Award. Most of us would surely think that only a lunatic would confuse like this the norms of economic exchange with the family norms of love and marriage.

Without norms our stories and poems would be incomprehensible. Eccentricity or individuality, the irreducibly unique or strange, can be perceived as such only in relation to norms and normative behavior. The same holds for cheating or bullying, misogyny, self-aggrandizement, self-destruction, or any attitude or action we consider too much or too little.

9

Another point: not only is public and private life drenched in norms, and not only are these norms mutable, changing as our circumstances change, but they are also anything but monolithic. They do not arrange themselves in easily apprehended hierarchies of value. And often they compete for our allegiance. Think of how many of our favorite stories and poems originate in or revolve around the tension or conflict between competing norms, ideals, or values: the bonds of family with the bonds of state (as in *Antigone*), or religious allegiance with biological attachment (as in Ben Jonson's famous elegy for his son). Think of Hamlet or Orestes caught between equally bad alternatives, unable to appease one parent without enraging or betraying the other. How to adjudicate the value of competing norms without diminishing either norm's importance, or minimizing the cost of choosing this one over that, is, I would argue, the ongoing open-ended work of poetic decorum, of decorum not defined by any particular set of norms but by the site-specific, unanticipated on-the-fly adjustments one makes among or between norms, needs, values, in each particular act of writing or living.

10

In section 4 of Wallace Stevens's "Sunday Morning," about halfway through the poem, the speaker counters his female avatar's fear of death and change, her emotional attachment to the consolations of religion and the hope of an afterlife, with this amazing periodic sentence:

There is not any haunt of prophecy,
Nor any old chimera of the grave,
Neither the golden underground, nor isle
Melodious, where spirits gat them home,
Nor visionary south, nor cloudy palm
Remote on heaven's hill, that has endured
As April's green endures, or will endure
Like her remembrance of awakened birds,
Or her desire for June and evening, tipped
By the consummation of the swallow's wings.

The rhetorical argument couldn't be clearer: biblical and pagan visions of an eternal afterlife have come and gone, while seasonal recurrence, memory, and desire in the widest sense are permanent features of human experience. What this paraphrase leaves out, however, is the tone of the sentence, the suggestion of nostalgia for the very thing the sentence is dismissing, the emotional attachment to an idea of heaven or some imperishable bliss, which the secular intellect rejects. That attachment is present in the subtly modulated musicality of the blank verse, with clauses sometimes coinciding with the line, sometimes breaking the line up into longer or shorter units, as the caesura shifts to different positions, falling in one line in the middle of the second foot ("Melodious, where"), or after the fourth foot in another ("golden underground, nor isle"), or as in the penultimate line in the middle of the fifth foot ("evening, tipped"); these formal elements vary our experience of the line while the line itself is always heard, always audible; add to this the incantatory repetition of "nor" and "neither," the fondly archaic biblical inversions and turns of phrase, the gorgeous modifiers, never mind the internal rhymes ("old," "golden," "melodious"), assonantal and consonantal chiming ("grave," "gat," "ground") all throughout the passage, and you can sense how the feeling is continuously tilting back fondly, yearningly, toward what the argument is unambiguously rejecting.

Compare this sentence to Paul's injunction in Romans 8:37: "For I am sure that neither death, nor life, nor angels, nor principalities, nor things present, nor things to come, nor powers, nor height, nor depth, nor any thing else in all creation, will be able to separate us from the love of God in Christ Jesus our Lord." Stevens's sentence mirrors the proliferation of negative noun clauses in the sentence by Paul, even as it turns the Pauline argument on its head. But Paul's tone is undivided—the piling up of negatively offered nouns, not one of which is modi fied or qualified in any way whatsoever, only invests the long verb clause that concludes the sentence with more absolute authority. Doctrine tolerates no qualification: God, after all, gave us the Ten Commandments, not the ten suggestions. And just as doctrine, according to Paul, should regulate every aspect of the self, so here in this sentence it regulates every aspect of the writing. Decorum as maidservant to doctrine permits no tonal waffling, no lingering wistfulness, no buyer's remorse, as I think there is in the sentence by Stevens.

The poetic decorum of "Sunday Morning," however, extends beyond the imperative to accept the world in all its mutability. It qualifies its own this-world affirmation by recognizing, even if only on the level of tone, the emotional cost of and resistance to the very acceptance the poem advocates. Poetic decorum as a subspecies of decorum proper can be thought of as devotion to the truth with all its jagged contradictory edges—adapting language to experience so as to make the fullest possible response, to register and embrace the most inclusive rendering of life.

11

The romantics were right to reject or balk at their neoclassical forebears. A lot of the poetry we think of when we think of the eighteenth century had become too polite, too beautiful. Much as I love Johnson, Dryden, and Pope ("The Vanity of Human Wishes," "Mac Flecknoe," and "The Rape of the Lock" are still fun to read) and consider their satire just as sharp and timely now as it was then, there is something deadening to a modern sensibility in the mix of closed couplet with periphrastic diction, which, after a while, comes to seem almost offensively elegant. This oppressively relentless sheen is most apparent in Pope's translation of the *Iliad*, where Homer's directness and grit is scrubbed off and made presentable to polite society. As Adam Nicolson writes in *Why Homer Matters*, "Where, for example, Homer had said simply, 'the shepherd's heart is glad,' Pope had written, 'The conscious swains, rejoicing in the sight/ Eye the blue vault, and bless the useful light.'" But it's the battle scenes especially that show just how ill matched Pope's manner is to Homer's realism.

In book 20, in a merciless rampage after the death of Patroclus, Achilles is cutting a wide, bloody swath through enemy lines when a young Trojan soldier he's subdued embraces his knees and begs for his life. Here's the scene in Richmond Lattimore's translation:

> Now Tros, Alastor's son, he had come against Achilleus'
>   knees,
> to catch them and be spared and his life given to him
> if Achilleus might take pity upon his youth and not
>   kill him;

fool, he did not see there would be no way to persuade him,
since this was a man with no sweetness in his heart, and
    not kindly
but in a strong fury; now Tros with his hands reaching
for the knees, bent on supplication, but he stabbed with his
    sword at the liver
so that the liver was torn from its place, and from it the
    black blood
drenched the fold of his tunic and his eyes were shrouded
    in darkness
as the life went . . .

Here is Pope's translation:

In vain his youth, in vain his beauty pleads:
In vain he begs thee, with a suppliant's moan
To spare a form and age so like thy own!
Unhappy boy! No prayer, no moving art
E'er bent that fierce inexorable heart!
While yet he trembled at his knees, and cried,
The ruthless falchion oped his tender side;
The panting liver pours a flood of gore,
That drowns his bosom till he pants no more.

Lattimore's rough accentual verse and earthy no-nonsense
diction seem more suitable for Homer's ferocious realism, the
physicality of his description, than Pope's breathy rhetoric,
silky-smooth pentameters, and catchy rhymes. Compare Pope's
Fred Astaire–like suave antithesis of "the panting liver . . .
pants no more" with Lattimore's simple and cool directness
("the liver was torn from its place, and from it the black blood /
drenched the fold of his tunic"), and it's hard not to think that

Pope has showed up for a street fight wearing a tux and top hat, twirling a cane.

12

Pope's Homer was a huge success when it appeared early in the eighteenth century. It sold more copies, relatively speaking, than *Fifty Shades of Gray* sold here in the US a few years ago. Samuel Johnson called Pope's *Iliad* "a treasure of poetical elegances." Elegance, of course, as Adam Nicolson says, is precisely the problem. After the violent upheavals of the previous century, the Reformation, the Puritan revolution, the Counter-Reformation, one can see why a strict decorum enforcing a stable, harmonious, and uniform elegance would have been embraced so eagerly by eighteenth-century English readers and writers. At the same time, one can also see how contrary those rules and regulations were to the decorum that Homer's commitment to unvarnished truth required.

Times change; tastes change. Social practices and the norms they generate are never fixed, even while every culture acts as if they are, presenting as eternal its own historically particular solutions to the problems it faces. But isn't it also true that Lattimore's translation is better than Pope's not only or primarily because it's closer to us in time; not only because his accentual verse is more like the free verse most of us read and write; but more importantly because it approximates more decorously, more sensitively in English the visceral immediacy of Homer's ancient Greek? Times change, but not to the exclusion of any and all continuities in human experience. If that were true, we couldn't read, much less appreciate and be moved by, any literature older than the here and now, never mind works as old as the *Iliad* and *The Epic of Gilgamesh*, poems in which human beings live and love and struggle for meaning under the shadow of death, in bodies infinitely vulnerable. In my view, Lattimore achieves a transhistorical decorum, a decorum constrained in some ways by his historical moment, but not entirely determined by it, at least not to the degree that Pope's translation is.

In a coffee shop the other day, I overheard a middle-aged woman say, "I can't help it, I always cry at baby showers, always." What a statement like this means is that the woman responds to any and all showers in exactly the same way, no matter what the particular circumstances happen to be; she carries into every baby shower a predetermined need to cry. There's nothing wrong with this, per se, but to always cry in the same way no matter what the particular shower calls for is to make the occasion itself incidental to one's experience of it. Our reactions should depend on the moment itself and any number of other factors—whether you're the parent of the expectant mother or a sibling, or a friend, for instance, or the pregnant woman's childless aunt, or whether you yourself have children, or maybe just discovered that you're expecting too. Sometimes maybe you should cry; sometimes, maybe if the circumstance calls for it, you should laugh, or pout or protest or just sit in silence, or in the course of the shower maybe you should do all of the above. But to always cry, always, is to impose an emotion on a moment whether or not the emotion is appropriate. In his translation of the *Iliad*, Pope is like this woman. He unilaterally imposes his particular style of writing, the conventions and mores of his time, onto a poem that calls for a very different kind of verbal response. He in effect is cut off from the poem he is translating. Or rather he is translating Homer into the eighteenth century without at the same time translating himself back into Homer.

13

What connects us to the widest range of feeling, to the richness of experience itself, is what I've been calling poetic decorum, a mental poise or readiness that promotes access to more experiential possibility than we otherwise would have. It is antithetical to unilateral and exclusive forms of thought and feeling; it is the enemy of sentimentality, as James Baldwin defines it in "Everybody's Protest Novel." "Sentimentality," he says, "the ostentatious parading of excessive and spurious emotion, is the mark of dishonesty, the inability to feel; the wet eyes of the sentimentalist betray his aversion to experience, his fear of life, his arid heart; and it is always, therefore, the signal of secret and violent inhumanity, the mask of cruelty." Sentimentality is, Baldwin suggests, the replacement of the complications of experience with a palatable lie, a lie that's palatable because it cuts the human figure down to size, simplifies it, categorizes it, abstracts it from the unmanageable complexities of circumstance in the interest of control or the illusion of control. The connection between sentimentality and racism and bigotry suggests that what we do when we sentimentalize our own experience is similar to what we do when we see another person through the lens of a reductive stereotype: in both cases, we replace the concrete truth with a bloodless abstraction. Using Baldwin's definition, we can say that sentimentality is bigotry internalized, and bigotry is sentimentality writ large.

Decorum is that imaginative faculty that resists these kinds of life-denying abstractions and simplifications. A refined and sharpened sense of decorum guides us as we write and revise our stories and poems, enables us to determine as exactly as possible in each improvisatory moment of composition how much is too much, how much is not enough. It's what good stories and poems activate and enliven in the minds and hearts of attentive readers. Decorum commits us to a vision of truth as fullness, fullness of thought, fullness of feeling ever engaged with and responsive to fullness of life.

Convention and Mysticism: Dickinson, Hardy, Williams

A guy falls into a well; as he plummets down the well shaft he grabs hold of a root, breaking his fall, and dangles there, terrified. He looks down into the black abyss below him, then up at the tiny circle of blue sky overhead. "Anybody up there?!" he shouts. "Anybody up there?!" A bright light fills the circle, and out of the light a voice booms—"I AM the Lord thy God, let go of the root and I shall save thee." The guy looks down into the blackness, thinks for a moment, and then looks up again and shouts, "Anybody *else* up there?!"

Like all jokes, what makes this one funny is the turn it takes. What begins as a sacred parable pivots in the punch line into something utterly profane. The spiritual pattern the story leads us to expect (spiritual salvation requiring trust in things unseen) deflates into something all too ordinary and of this world (physical survival at any cost).

Another way to describe this would be to say the joke depends on our knowing the sacred narrative it solicits and then subverts. It works by upending the convention or norm of expectation. By evoking and then breaking the pattern of something old and familiar (biblical story, conversion narrative), it generates the sensation of something new and different. Without the foil of some already established convention or norm of expectation, there is less chance of surprise. And it follows from this that the more conventions or patterns a joke or any work of art can put into play, the greater opportunity there is for meaningful surprise.

Here's a famous poem by Emily Dickinson that flips frames on us the way the joke does. The poem is a kind of joke, at least on the speaker's and reader's spiritual expectations:

I heard a Fly buzz – when I died –
The Stillness in the Room
Was like the Stillness in the Air –
Between the Heaves of Storm –

The Eyes around – had wrung them dry –
And Breaths were gathering firm
For that last Onset –when the King
Be witnessed – in the Room –

I willed my Keepsakes – Signed away
What portion of me be
Assignable – and then it was
There interposed a Fly –

With Blue – uncertain – stumbling Buzz –
Between the light – and me –
And then the Windows failed – and then
I could not see to see –

The arc of the poem describes the speaker's contracting vision, moving in from the hushed room and the depersonalized eyes and breaths around a deathbed, to the speaker's failing eyesight/windows, then into the mind's last guttering of consciousness. She is expecting or hoping for Christ "the King" to come and escort her to a better place. The religious yearning is ironically intensified by the poem's meter, which is hymn meter, the conventional music of such yearning. The speaker is hoping for a good death, a death that leads to heaven, the sign of which would be the King's arrival, but all that shows up is a fly, coming, one assumes, for its portion of what the speaker has just signed away, which of course would be her body. The language of spiritual faltering implicit in the diction of the last five lines—the fly's stumbling, uncertain buzz, the window failing, and the speaker unable to see to see—turns on its head the prototypical salvation narrative celebrated in so many hymns: "Amazing grace! How sweet the sound / That saved a wretch like me! / I was once was lost, but now am found; / Was blind but now I see." This reversal of expectation suggests two equally disquieting possibilities: either the King does not show up and the speaker's damned, not saved; or, worse, the King does show up but turns out to be a fly, not a god, which means we live in a material universe in which there is no god, no heaven or hell (which perhaps is why the dead speaker describes what it's like to die but tells us nothing at all about what it's like being dead), a universe of death whose king is the fly, a carrion feeder.

On the level of syllable and foot, the metrical form reinforces the speaker's sly questioning of the tenets of belief, the reversal of expectation, for the form, again, is hymn meter, the conventional music of Christian piety. Dickinson doesn't merely adopt that conventional music, though; she roughens it with off-rhymes and with subtle enjambment between the third and fourth quatrains, and more noticeably with medial caesurae that sometimes fall between feet and sometimes in the middle of a given foot ("buzz | when," "my Keep | sakes – Signed," "uncer | tain – stum | bling Buzz"), interrupting the momentum of the cadence and muting our experience of the form. To adjust a meter so integrally associated with religious faith, with conventions of worship, to express such a delicately blasphemous idea is like using a limerick to express a devastating sorrow ("My mother's now dead from bone cancer. / When the tumor swelled up then they lanced her"). That Dickinson pulls it off so subtly, so movingly, torquing the micro-elements of the music without falling into inadvertent bathos ("But the tumor still spread / All the way to her head, / And the pain made her dance like a dancer") is no small part of the poem's achievement.

Any good poem, metrical or not, depends on an expressive, mutually entailing dance of something fixed with something changed. By *pattern* we mean more than repeated arrangements of accented and unaccented syllables; we also mean rhyme, line lengths, stanzas, even sentences, and how sentences are drawn through lines and stanzas. In every case, the creation of surprise is closely tied to any number of recurring structures.

And as the joke and the Dickinson poem demonstrate, this is not just a sonic principle but a semantic one as well. Repetition with modification is a fundamental means by which a writer can dramatize or vocalize a felt change of consciousness. Metaphors that discover similarities (repeated properties) between dissimilar objects, linguistic or imagistic motifs in which the same or similar word or image is repeated in different contexts in order to dramatize change and continuity, words recurring in different grammatical forms—these are all expressions of the same basic principle of interdependence between pattern and variation, the familiar and the new. As in the old Cahn and Van Heusen song "Love and Marriage," they go together like a horse and carriage—in the Sinatra version, "This I tell you, brother, / You can't have one without the other."

I could pick any poem in any form to illustrate this principle, but for starters, here's Thomas Hardy's famous poem "The Oxen," which employs a looser version of the same meter as "I heard a Fly buzz" but to very different effect:

Christmas Eve, and twelve of the clock.
    "Now they are all on their knees,"
An elder said as we sat in a flock
    By the embers in hearthside ease.

We pictured the meek mild creatures where
    They dwelt in their strawy pen,
Nor did it occur to one of us there
    To doubt they were kneeling then.

So fair a fancy few would weave
    In these years! Yet, I feel,
If someone said on Christmas Eve,
    "Come; see the oxen kneel,

"In the lonely barton by yonder coomb,
    Our childhood used to know,"
I should go with him in the gloom,
    Hoping it might be so.

Before looking in detail at "The Oxen," I want to offer a warning about the sort of dangers that often attend metrical analyses.

Discussions of meter and formal strategies of any kind can easily degenerate into sentimental impressionism if one isn't careful to connect form to content, style to subject matter, metrical properties to semantic meaning. No form or style is inherently significant or meaningful in isolation from the meaning of the words themselves. I remember Cunningham discussing an analysis of John Keats's "La Belle Dame Sans Merci" by a famous critic, in which the critic claimed that the feeling of desolation and bereavement of the last line was a direct consequence of the heavily stressed syllables in the last foot: "And no birds sing." The critic made no mention of words themselves, their particular meaning, and how the narrative prepares us for that feeling of tragic loss. Rather, he claimed that the effect was caused by the sound of the last three equally stressed monosyllabic words themselves (the accented syllable of the first foot followed by the spondee [or heavily stressed iamb] of the second), as if that weight of feeling existed inside the weight of the stress, the sound, the rhythm, independent of semantic meaning. If that were true, Cunningham remarked, then presumably the poem would convey the same feeling if Keats had used different words that replicated the same sound, the same cluster of three monosyllabic words, all equally stressed: "And no cows moo."

Anybody *else* up there?

Or to take another example, according to this way of thinking, there'd be no difference whatsoever if Edgar Allan Poe had decided to stick with his original choice of bird for his most famous poem: "Quoth the parrot never more."

Dodged a bullet there.

Metrical effects depend on meaning, on context. So do many of the terms we use for our experience of form in general. So when I say a stanza or quatrain is closed or open, I'm treating the terms as wholly dependent on the particular poem in which they occur.

"Church Monuments," by George Herbert, beautifully illustrates the context-dependent nature of what we call open or closed effects. The poem is a religious meditation. While the soul focuses on her devotion to God and heaven, the body meditates down in the catacombs, where it concentrates on death and mutability:

> While that my soul repairs to her devotion,
> Here I entomb my flesh, that it betimes
> May take acquaintance of this heap of dust;
> To which the blast of death's incessant motion,
> Fed with the exhalation of our crimes,
> Drives all at last. Therefore I gladly trust
>
> My body to this school, that it may learn
> To spell his elements, and find his birth
> Written in dusty heraldry and lines;
> Which dissolution sure doth best discern,
> Comparing dust with dust, and earth with earth.
> These laugh at jet and marble put for signs,
>
> To sever the good fellowship of dust,
> And spoil the meeting. What shall point out them,
> When they shall bow, and kneel, and fall down flat
> To kiss those heaps, which now they have in trust?
> Dear flesh, while I do pray, learn here thy stem
> And true descent; that when thou shalt grow fat,
>
> And wanton in thy cravings, thou mayst know
> That flesh is but the glass, which holds the dust
> That measures all our time; which also shall
> Be crumbled into dust. Mark here below
> How tame these ashes are, how free from lust,
> That thou mayst fit thyself against thy fall.

This is a poem about instability within apparent stability. The church monuments erected to celebrate the family name, that invest that name with an illusion of permanence, of imperishability, are themselves disintegrating like the perishable bodies they contain ("What shall point out them, / When they shall bow, and kneel, and fall down flat"). The figure introduced in the final stanza that captures the mutability of all material things is the hourglass, which, like the sand running through it, is also crumbling. Think of the stanza as the sonic manifestation of the monuments themselves, and think of the syntax, as it is drawn through the lines and stanzas, as the sonic equivalent of the sand. And then notice how the enjambments proliferate in the first four lines of the final six-line stanza. Not only that, but if you read these lines from caesura to caesura, you get four more iambic pentameter units laid across the pentameter units of the lines themselves. The rhythm consequently quickens, diminishing without entirely destroying our experience of the line. But even as we experience the line we can't help but hear that second pentameter unit stealthily running from caesura to caesura, threatening the linear structure.

The apparently stable line, like the apparently stable glass, is holding the very forces wearing or eroding it away. The relation between sentence and line in the previous three stanzas is more "closed," and when there is enjambment in one line, either the line that follows has no pause or pauses less emphatically or, if the pause is longer, the unit reaching from one caesura to the other is either tetrameter or hexameter, with one exception— "that it may learn / to spell his elements." Nowhere till the last stanza do we get four consecutive run-overs creating that double pentameter effect. The sudden openness coincident with the image of the hourglass has been prepared for, has been set up by being set off against the way the sentence courses through the lines of earlier stanzas.

On the other hand, if you compare even the most open line in "Church Monuments" to the short-line free verse of William Carlos Williams, in which the line often cuts into the sentence after a preposition or a pronoun, the "open" Herbert line will seem safely closed. *Closure* and *openness*, in other words, are relative terms, and their effects are wholly dependent not just on the formal properties of the poems in which they appear but also on the poem's semantic, rhetorical, and vocal properties, in addition to the expectations a reader brings to the work itself, his or her familiarity with poetry in general or modern poetry in particular, and the innovations that poets like Williams were experimenting with in relation to prosody and line, and what a poem was or could be.

With respect to the metrical conventions of "The Oxen," then, the first thing to notice is that it's written in hymn or ballad meter—four-line stanzas (quatrains) of alternating four-beat and three-beat lines, rhymed *abab*. The first two quatrains are closed—that is, the end of the quatrain coincides with the end of the sentence. The third quatrain is open, relative to the first two, in that the sentence extends beyond the border of the four-line unit. Metrically, the first two quatrains of "The Oxen" are unusual. While the majority of feet are iambic, every line has at least one or two anapestic substitutions, and the first foot of the first line is monosyllabic, followed by two iambs and a final anapest: "Christmas Eve, and twelve of the clock." The pattern of alternating anapestic and iambic feet is broken in the third quatrain, in which every foot is iambic, though with varying degrees of stress among accented and unaccented syllables. Then Hardy returns to the anapestic substitutions or some facsimile thereof in the concluding quatrain.

Of course, none of this is very interesting on its own, or even meaningful in isolation from the content. With respect to content, the first thing to notice is the temporal structure, how the poem moves from past to present, from childhood to adulthood, and from faith to skepticism. The speaker recalls sitting with other children on Christmas evening while the elders tell them that the oxen too are kneeling in celebration of the birth of Christ. The innocence of the children, their unquestioned faith in what the elders tell them, and the sensation of unity between the supernatural and natural, the human and the animal, is suggested by the metaphors that animalize the children ("as we sat in a flock") and humanize the animals ("Now they are all on their knees").

As the present replaces the past, adult skepticism replaces belief. But the important thing to notice is not the skepticism per se but the elegiac tone expressing emotional attachment to what the speaker intellectually disbelieves. Whereas in childhood he took on faith what the elders told him, as an adult empiricist he needs proof; he can believe only what he sees with his own eyes, so he imagines going out to the barn to see if the oxen are really kneeling. The simplicity of childhood gives way to adult complexity, a complexity the very syntax embodies. Just as his vision is no longer contained by the stories he grew up with, so the syntax in the third quatrain (again, relative to the first two) is no longer contained by the four-line stanza. The very structure of the sentence too enacts the change of point of view. The relatively simple sentences in the first two quatrains become in the third and fourth a long, conditional sentence. Belief for the speaker is now conditional, not unconditional, and the implied premise of this particular conditional is that, of course, no one nowadays, in such a skeptical age, would ever invite him to go see if the oxen are kneeling. The remoteness of that folk belief from the present-day world of fact is nicely captured by the heavy alliteration in stanza 3, which in this instance calls attention to the fancifulness or artificiality of the belief, that it's just a fancy, not a fact, and by the archaic diction in stanza 4.

Again, what makes the "open" quatrain feel significantly open is the pattern of closed quatrains that precede it, and the coincidence of those closed quatrains in *this* poem with childhood innocence, with taking things on faith. What makes the complex sentence of the last two quatrains meaningful, what even gives it the feeling of complexity, are, first, the coincidence of that sentence with the complex perspective of the adult speaker, the unlikely thought experiment he conducts, of someone inviting him out to see if the oxen are kneeling; and second, the simpler sentences of the first two quatrains about childhood that precede it. And what makes those anapests feel like sonic extensions of the speaker's lost faith and childhood innocence is the drumbeat of iambs that replace them in the third quatrain, iambs which are the normative foot in the poem, the underlying but always audible grid over which those variations play and in relation to which they have their meaning.

Think of the metrical norm as the sonic symbol of a reality in which there is no divinity, and the rhythm as the sonic symbol of the speaker's emotional longing for or persistent attachment to what he knows is false. Both sonic symbols are prominent in the concluding quatrain, especially in the last line, which begins with a trochee followed by two iambs. What the trochaic substitution in the first foot does, though, is create the illusion of an anapest, because the accented first syllable ("hope") is followed by two unaccented syllables leading to the accented "might." As we move from first syllable to fourth (from "hope" to "might"), we recapitulate the movement of the entire poem. The ghost of the earlier anapestic line, in which childhood belief still haunts the speaker, gives way here to the speaker's own resistance to that belief: the speaker is indulging in a fantasy while reminding himself that a fantasy is all it is. So the reversed first foot, in this instance, because of the semantic/metrical coincidences leading up to it, conveys the feeling both of resistance, an intellectual pulling back or reversal, and of indulgence, an emotional giving in, hence the anapestic illusion.

Norms of expectation, pattern, and convention, of experiential, linguistic, and literary associations established by what's repeated over time, provide the necessary if not sufficient conditions for our experience and understanding of what is constantly changing, on and off the page. Isn't the very concept of "news" itself inversely proportionate to an event's expectedness? And if it's not too much of a stretch, how do we recognize individual talent except against the background of some tradition? One might even say that the enemy of an ongoing, vital tradition is the very predictability that would freeze it in place, and not the innovations that would keep it responsive to a changing world.

And yet many poets of my generation have assumed, in theory if not in practice, that any and all conventions or predetermined forms (and by this I mean not just poetic forms but grammatical forms as well) are inherently mechanical and stale, and thus enemies of individual expression. This is an unfortunate legacy of modernism, or at least of an incomplete grasp of what modernism stood for. Ironically, nobody better understood how intimately tradition and individual talent are entwined than many of the very poets we invoke to justify this false dichotomy.

From the modern period, no American poet is more associated with experiment and innovation than William Carlos Williams. Like nearly all the modern poets, Williams promoted disjunction and fragmentation, once even claiming that the reason we prefer the previews of coming attractions to the movies themselves is because the trailers, in giving us only the most intense, disjointed moments of a story, eliminate what he calls "the banality of sequence."

Yet despite Williams's anticonventional, antitraditional stance, in his poems, early and late, if not always in his essays, he was exquisitely attuned to the many ways in which convention and originality are interdependent, mutually entailing, not mutually exclusive. His best poems play off some unconventional perception against an implied conventional screen. Sometimes the conventions are experiential, as in "Sorrow," where he sets up a scene of a father walking home from work, enjoying the sassafras leaves and the evening light, and then when he's greeted by the happy shouts of his children he is crushed, not exhilarated, as we'd expect. Sometimes the conventions are literary or formal, as in "Queen Anne's Lace," Williams's rewriting of Shakespeare's sonnet 130, "My mistress' eyes are nothing like the sun"—crossing images of woman and flower, Williams begins with a series of negatives, just as Shakespeare does, in order to explode conventional assumptions about female sexuality, passivity, and purity. This woman/flower is "not so white as / anemone petals, nor / so smooth nor so remote a thing"; she isn't sexually weak or passive but rather "takes the field by force"; aroused and arousing, she embodies "a pious wish for whiteness / gone over," that is, gotten beyond, "or nothing."

Likewise, in the first poem of Williams's great experimental book *Spring and All,* his pastoral landscape of creative renewal is American/urban, not European/rural, and the month is March, an even crueler month than April, on a cold, cloudy, windy day by the road to a contagious hospital:

under the surge of the blue
mottled clouds driven from the
northeast—a cold wind. Beyond, the
waste of broad, muddy fields
brown with dried weeds, standing and fallen

patches of standing water
the scattering of tall trees

All along the road the reddish
purplish, forked, upstanding, twiggy
stuff of bushes and small trees
with dead, brown leaves under them
leafless vines—

Lifeless in appearance, sluggish
dazed spring approaches—

They enter the new world naked,
cold, uncertain of all
save that they enter. All about them
the cold, familiar wind—

Now the grass, tomorrow
the stiff curl of wildcarrot leaf

One by one objects are defined—
It quickens: clarity, outline of leaf

But now the stark dignity of
entrance—Still, the profound change
has come upon them: rooted, they
grip down and begin to awaken

From our past experience of spring poems, we expect a pastoral landscape, vaguely Italianate—instead we get New Jersey. Anybody *else* up there?

The Virgilian renewal, though, which pastoral is supposed to celebrate, does, in fact, take place exactly as it should and yet is all the more surprising because it emerges where we least expect it. What makes the poem so original is that it manages to celebrate the return of spring in a way that avoids the clichés both of the pastoral convention and of the dystopian irony of Eliot's "Waste Land," which by the mid-1920s had already become a convention in its own right. Williams ironizes Eliot's irony by invoking it to show how far he's gone beyond it into what finally is a wholly unironic, even somewhat traditional celebration of creative energy in the American scene as well as in the self.

Or consider the following poem, "Portrait of a Lady":

Your thighs are apple trees
whose blossoms touch the sky.
Which sky? The sky
where Watteau hung a lady's
slipper. Your knees
are a southern breeze—or
a gust of snow. Agh! What
sort of man was Fragonard?
—as if that answered
anything. Ah, yes—below
the knees, since the tune
drops that way, it is
one of those white summer days,
the tall grass of your ankles
flickers upon the shore—

Which shore?—
The sand clings to my lips—
Which shore?
Agh, petals maybe. How
should I know?
Which shore? Which shore?
I said petals from an apple tree.

I don't think, as some do, that Williams is alluding to Henry James's great novel *Portrait of a Lady*. I think rather he's playing with the conventions of portrait painting, with its devotion to the physical image of the person being painted, to the face especially. When we bring these expectations to the poem, we notice right away that the speaker/poet/painter is less interested in this woman's literal appearance than in his own poetic abilities. She seems almost incidental to his desire to show off his metaphorical skill and his knowledge of art, which turns out to be shaky at best. The heart of the poem has less to do with the "portrait" the speaker is trying to paint in words, which are loosely based on an eighteenth-century rococo painting, than with the woman's implied interruptions, her refusal to let the speaker's tune "drop" where it will. Well, if he's going to compare her to a famous painting, he'd better know whose painting it is, which he doesn't. And what kind of man would put a girl on a swing and place a voyeur (the painter himself?) under her so he can look up her dress(!)?

Anybody *else* up there?

He wants to write his poem the way he wants to write it, but she won't let him. She corrects his misidentification of the painter, she asks annoying questions about where exactly the poem is taking place ("Which shore? Which shore?") and, worse, about the moral character of the painter. She affirms the biographical fallacy. In her view, the life of the artist, his moral character, should influence or inform our experience of the art. For the poet/speaker, though, art should be autonomous, self-enclosed, free of any and all extrinsic considerations. And as a poet, he should be left alone to write whatever he wants, however he wants to write it, responsible to nothing beyond his imagination. But for this lady, no artist, certainly not Williams himself, is ever only an artist, especially not if he's married to this woman and going to make her the subject of his work.

Williams does in the end give us a portrait of this lady, but not, as we're first led to expect, of her physical beauty. Instead, he paints a vivid picture of her character in and through the very poem she will not let him write, the poem she constantly interrupts. By means of her interruptions, we learn that she's a stickler for details, she's not someone to be bullied, and she knows more than he does about the very art he's trying to praise her with. By the end of the poem, the speaker is completely discombobulated by her refusal to let him wax poetic, by her insistence that he pay attention to her, not just to his idea of her (the thing itself, not the idea of the thing).

The lady is never literally described, but we end up with a memorable portrait of the kind of person she is. In a sly, self-deprecating way, Williams paints a wonderful and utterly unconventional portrait of a lady's character and of a marriage. The originality of the poem depends on our holding in mind a set of expectations about portrait painting, ekphrastic poetry, and the extravagant gestures of rococo art, as well as the newer but no less conventional disjunctive strategies of modernism. Williams establishes these multiple frames and patterns of expectation so he can show us how to look beyond them, to something never before expressed, at least not in the particular way that he expresses it here.

Sometime between 1910 and 1915, Williams composed an essay titled "Love and Service" that makes several assertions about the spiritual aim of poetry (and of all art, by extension) in the modern world. "Two things," Williams says, "we must avoid. We must not forget that we praise the unknown, the mystery about which nothing can be said; and second, that we praise in silence, the rest being but perishable signs. Then lest we mistake our signs for the reality let them be ever new, forever new for only by forever changing the sign can we learn to separate from it its meaning, the expression from the term, and so cease to be idolaters." The goal of art, Williams says, is the unknown, the mystery, which is less an entity than an action, a principle of change and disruptive transformation that is simultaneously hard to grasp and impossible not to feel. His insistence on the new and perpetual revolution as the goal of art is both quintessentially American and modern. It echoes Pound's slogan "Make it new," Emerson's call in "Nature" for an original relation to the universe, and beyond Emerson it harks back to the Puritans' distrust of mediation and idolatry. But Williams's sense of language as a system of perishable signs that displaces the realities and meanings it solicits looks forward as well to certain postmodern forms of skepticism. Of course, what qualifies this "postmodern" quality is the faith espoused here in some transcendent, genuinely life-enhancing principle, something that is both within and beyond language, separable from signs yet inextricably bound up with them, something that cannot be approached at all except through the very medium that obscures it.

Williams is often thought of as an iconoclast, someone who in the name of individual expression discards all predetermined forms and conventions. But what this picture distorts is the extent to which his unconventional perspective, as I have argued, depends on the very conventions it resists, in the same way that the unknown, the mystery, can be approached only through the perishable (socially constructed and therefore conventional) signs that displace it. Williams is also seldom thought of as a spiritual or religious poet. He is referred to most often as either an imagist or an objectivist poet who believed not in ideas but in things, that everything in life as well as art depends on looking carefully at a red wheelbarrow glazed with rain, and the green shards of a broken bottle between the walls of a hospital. Thus most readers overlook the extent to which Williams's poetry isn't really all that visual, or ever merely so, the extent to which his attention in his best poems is continually moving among things, never resting in any one thing, and that what motivates the movement is a love of surfaces that distrusts the surfaces it loves, including linguistic ones. This tension in Williams—between his desire to deflect attention from the conventionality of the sign to the mystery beyond it, and his recognition that the sign itself, the convention, the norm of expectation, is unavoidable, intractable, and the mystery in and of itself unspeakable—governs all aspects of his prosody. It shapes the very form and movement of his poems, which typically consist of short lines of free verse that cut into and break up long syntactical units. As the syntax courses through the lines, Williams formalizes his linguistic ambivalence by never letting our attention rest for very long on any one image or clause, by shifting our focus from the lines themselves to the restless, ever-changing energy among them.

Williams once remarked that poems are machines made out of words. This may seem inconsistent with his assertion that the purpose of poetry is to praise the unknown and mysterious in a way that somehow preserves by separating meaning from the very means by which that meaning is discovered and expressed. But for Williams, the quintessential American poet, the Protestant poet, distrustful of the very signs or conventions he cannot do without, the mystic and the pragmatic, the everyday and the unknown, are never far apart. In his view, poetry is a machine of words, of conventional signs, whose work is the controlled release of sacred (unconventional) energy. What good is the machine without the energy it runs on, the energy that enables it to work? And what good is the energy without the machine that gives it shape and texture and connects it to the world in which we live, the world we share with everybody else?

Why Write?

Some years ago I went to a child psychologist—if Henny Young-man had written this opening sentence, he would have added: "The Kid didn't do a thing for me." But I digress. The child psychologist I went to had recently tested one of my children for attention deficit disorder (ADD). When the results came back positive, he called my not-yet-ex-wife and me to suggest that we be tested too. There may be a genetic component to ADD, he said, and taking the test would not only reveal the extent to which we ourselves suffered from this condition but also enable us to better understand our child.

So we took the test. Turns out it's the only test I ever aced. As the doctor put it, in my case the results were salient.

"So, I'm ADD," I said. "What does that mean?"

"Well," he said, "according to the test, your ADD manifests itself in three ways: You have trouble starting tasks. You have trouble staying on task. And you have trouble finishing tasks."

"That pretty much covers it," I said. "But how do you explain the fact that I've written a number of books, and even today I spent several hours puzzling over a single sentence in a transla-tion I'm doing of a Greek tragedy?"

He said that it's not that people with ADD can't concen-trate on things they want to do, it's that they lack any ability to concentrate on anything that bores them. People with ADD have no tolerance for boredom. When I pointed out that I'd been teaching for over twenty-five years and seldom read a student paper that didn't make me want to drive an ice pick through my skull just to relieve the boredom but that I nonetheless returned each and every student paper in a timely fashion (even the ones I bothered to read—just kidding!), my soon to be ex-wife interjected: "But Alan, you can't remember the name of anyone you meet at a party."

"Sweetheart," I said, "that's called a greeting disorder."

"And," she continued, "even if I give you a list of groceries you come home with the wrong things, red peppers instead of tomatoes, bananas instead of squash."

"That's called being a guy," I said.

"And you don't hear five percent of what I tell you."

"That's called marriage." She wasn't amused.

Sensing the tension, the doctor asked, "So what do you think you want to do about this? How do we proceed?"

"With the ADD or with the marriage?"

Now it was his turn not to be amused. He went on to describe the kinds of medication I could take but then said he wasn't suggesting I do anything if I didn't think I was a problem to myself. People who grew up before this condition was named or treated have often found ingenious ways to compensate for their disabilities. Writing for me, he said, was a prime example of what he called compensatory behavior.

"Let me get this straight," I said. "I write books in order to make up for my inability to remember the names of the people I meet at a party, or because I come home from the grocery store with a red pepper instead of a tomato?"

"Well, not exactly," he said, but before he could explain exactly what he meant, the hour was up.

I don't know, maybe I was a tad defensive with the psychologist—you think?—and even a little miffed by his reduction of the art I love and have devoted my life to for the better part of almost forty years to a side effect of a neurological condition. At the same time, telling the story over, I can't help but ask myself, "Why do I write?" Is writing a compensation for psychological, emotional, or even neurological deficits? Do we write, as the old saying goes, because we can't do? Is art, as Freud believed, a kind of socially acceptable wish fulfillment for asocial infantile desires? A way of finding in imagination what we lost in life? A sublimation of sexual energy? A way of transmuting our hidden wishes or shameful secrets, our failures and losses and humiliations, into beautiful objects that win us wealth and admiration and all the sexual fulfillment that we put off in order to do the work in the first place? Why else get into the poetry racket? That I could even ask this question, even in jest, let alone attempt to make my way in the world by writing poetry is yet another manifestation of an abiding suspicion I've had for many years now that God put me on earth to disprove the stereotype that all Jews make money.

I once asked a very talented student of mine why she wanted to become a writer. Fame, she said. I want to be famous. And what did fame mean to her? It meant being able to check into the penthouse suite of a five-star hotel and totally trash the room and then be loved for it. This quintessentially American celebrity-driven fantasy is just the self-indulgent flipside of an older, time-honored messianic fantasy of the writer as unacknowledged cultural legislator. Seamus Heaney has written that poetry or great writing of any kind provides a culture with images adequate to its predicament. Who hasn't dreamed of providing everyone with images adequate to their predicament and being loved for it, and maybe even given loads of cash?

When we're in our teens and early twenties, maybe we all dream of becoming celebrated shamans of the heart, but that adolescent daydream doesn't begin to explain why we continue writing after the age of twenty-five or thirty, once we realize that the world isn't exactly rushing out to take its marching orders from anything we've written.

I think of my dear friend Tim Dekin, a wonderful poet, who died a few years ago at the age of fifty-eight of pulmonary fibrosis. Tim's first full-length book, *Another Day on Earth*, was published posthumously in 2002 by TriQuarterly Books. Tim and I met at Stanford in 1975. Eventually we both ended up teaching in the Chicago area. He was a brilliant talker, a fabulous poet, and a very funny man who lost many years of his writing life to alcoholism. He held down a series of demanding low-paying jobs teaching freshman comp at various universities. After years of struggling unsuccessfully to find a publisher for his poetry, he wrote three very good novels that he likewise couldn't publish. In his last year of life, he returned to his first love, poetry, and finished his magnificent one book. Tethered to his oxygen machine, he drove from Chicago to Chapel Hill not long before he died so he and I could go over his new poems and put the manuscript together. My brother had just died, and I had broken up with my wife and was living in a basement apartment. Neither Tim nor I was in very good shape at the time, physically or otherwise.

During that visit, I told Tim a joke that a musician friend told me about the four stages in a musician's career: The first stage is "Who is Frederick Luby?" The second stage is "Get me Frederick Luby." The third stage is "Get me a young Frederick Luby!" And the fourth stage is "Who is Frederick Luby?" Tim laughed at the joke, then added ruefully, "I seem to have passed from stage one to stage four without ever having passed through stages two and three."

I cherish the memory of those few days with Tim, and I love the image of us in my dreary digs, Tim's poems spread out on the coffee table, Tim puffing on the oxygen tube the way he puffed on the forbidden cigars he still occasionally smoked, leaning over the poems, reading out passages, discussing them, rewriting them, the two of us beset with troubles, physical and emotional, but working rapturously nonetheless throughout the day and long into the night. What exactly were we doing? What lack were we trying to fill? What were we compensating for? Whatever it was, fame and fortune had absolutely nothing to do with it.

Which is not to say I don't desire fame and fortune. I do. I do. I'm not above them. In fact, I'm so far beneath them that I'd even happily forget fame if I could have just a little fortune. When I take a good hard look at the life I've chosen, I have to wonder how I've stuck it out as long as I have. For there's a Grand Canyon's worth of difference between the literary life I dreamed of as an adolescent and the life I found once I began to publish and actually live what passes for a literary life.

I remember thinking in my teens and early twenties that if I could only publish a poem in a magazine, any magazine, I'd feel fulfilled and validated and wildly happy. And then I got my first publication. And I was happy for a day or so, until the bill arrived for the printing cost, and then I thought if I could only get a poem into a real journal, a magazine that pays, I'd feel validated and happy, and when that happened, I began to feel the need to publish in the *Atlantic Monthly* or the *New Yorker*, magazines that someone other than my fellow writers may have heard of, and eventually when that happened I believed that only publishing a book with a reputable press would make me feel as if I'd earned the right to call myself a poet. And then I published a book, and the resounding silence and inattention of the world (it's my books that suffer from attention deficit disorder, not me) made me feel that the only measure of my poetic worth would be to get a book reviewed somewhere by someone I didn't know, someone who wasn't related to me, and when that occurred, and pleased me, and the pleasure passed, I thought that only winning a big book award could quell this anxiety about my literary worth. I didn't realize how preoccupied I was with literary recognition till one day I overheard my seven-year-old son negotiating with my five-year-old daughter over who got to hold the TV's remote control. He said, "Izzy, if you give me the controller I'll give you a Pulitzer Prize." I've been at this long enough to know that even if God himself, the Lord Almighty, hallowed be His name, came down from heaven and gave me a big fat kiss on the back of the brain, I'd probably shrug it off: "What? That's it? For years you don't write, you don't call, and now all I get is a lousy kiss?"

Don't get me wrong. Acclaim of any kind is wonderful, except when it goes to someone else. But even at its best, that sort of "reward" or "recognition" is like cotton candy: it looks ample enough until you put it in your mouth, then it evaporates. All taste and no nourishment.

Then there's the thrill of dealing with editors. By way of illustration, let me tell you a story. In 1976, before I'd published anything, I wrote a long-windy poem called "Fathers and Sons." I sent it to the journal *Quarterly West*. The editor sent the poem back with a note suggesting I rewrite the middle two sections and resubmit it. I knew from watching the editors of *Sequoia*, the Stanford literary journal, that all editors are overworked and underpaid and can't possibly read everything that crosses their desk with keen attention. So I waited six months and sent the poem back unchanged with a letter thanking the editor for his suggestions, all of which I said I took. I even thanked him for his help and said that even if he didn't accept the poem I was still in his debt, for his suggestions had made the poem new to me again, more like what I initially envisioned when I started writing it. Within days I received a letter from the editor accepting the poem and commending me for my professionalism.

In 1997, at the Bread Loaf Writers Conference, I participated in an editors' roundtable. At the time I was the editor of the University of Chicago's Phoenix Poets series, and I told this story in order to make the point that writers need to treat what editors tell them with a healthy dose of skepticism. Don't presume an editor is smart just because he or she is an editor. Editors should have to earn their authority by reading what you send them with intelligence and imagination, and in any case they themselves, the writers, ought always to be the ultimate arbiters of what they do. Editors, I said, are mostly obstacles to get around. I returned to Bread Loaf two years later, and one of the students stopped to thank me for my advice back in 1997. He said he followed it and it worked like a charm. What do you mean, I asked. What advice? "Well, I got a poem back from *Boulevard*, and the editor suggested I do a major rewrite. So I waited six months like you said and sent it back with a letter thanking him for his time and help, and he accepted the poem."

The moral of this story isn't that editors are fools, though some are. The moral isn't that you should con your way into print, though if you do more power to you. Rather, the moral is you needn't listen to everything an editor tells you. The moral is you need to be cynical about publishing in order not to be cynical about writing, in order to protect and preserve the deeply private joy of doing the work itself. (I'll say more about that private joy in a moment.) I know it's hard, sometimes impossible, to keep the po biz out of the poetry, to keep the anxieties and injustices of trying to publish from contaminating your own relationship to what you do. It's hard to find the proper balance between the arrogance we need to keep on writing, the arrogance that assumes that we have something worth saying and that we're smart enough to learn what someone's smart enough to teach us, and the humility we also need in order to grow and develop, the humility that knows that we cannot nurture and refine our gifts without the help of others, that other people including editors can sometimes tell us things we need to hear. Too much arrogance and not enough humility, and we close ourselves off from the world, and nothing new comes in and we eventually become imitators of ourselves, turning what at one time were discoveries into mannerisms. And too much humility and not enough arrogance and we lose our center of gravity and find ourselves at the mercy of everyone else's opinion. Striking the right balance between humility and arrogance is another exhausting and often frustrating aspect of the writing life.

And then there's the frustration that surrounds the work itself, the work we've already done and the work we want to do. The dissatisfactions we often feel with older work, not to mention the frustrations we often feel with what we're writing now as well as the anxieties we feel about what we may do next, put me in mind of the old joke about the Jew who's shipwrecked on a desert island. Twenty years later, he's discovered, but before he leaves he wants to show his saviors the three synagogues he's built. "Over there," he says, "is the synagogue I used to go to. Over there's the synagogue I go to now. And over there, that synagogue, I wouldn't set foot in." I know this is really a joke about class and status, and the need to feel superior to something. But

I do think the more we refine our abilities, the more embarrassing our older work becomes. That is, if we're truly lucky, we'll despise our early work. If we're lucky, we'll feel as if nearly everything but what we're writing now was written by someone else we'd rather not be seen in public with. And if we're lucky, what we're writing now won't compare with what we'll write ten years from now. That's the price we pay for getting better. The problem is the better we get at writing, the better we get at imagining getting even better. So the discrepancy between the writer we are and the writer we want to be only widens as we improve. To flourish as an artist requires a tolerance for frustration and inadequacy and a deepening sense of failure.

And that's the good news. Now let's consider the effect of what we write on those we write about. Over the years, I learned the hard way that no one wants to give up narrative control over his or her life. Yet my theory's always been that if I try to tell the truth, if I have no ax to grind and write about others in a spirit of forgiveness, curiosity, and understanding, then no one should be upset by anything I say. Well, so much for theory. Even the most affectionate portrait of a loved one, the most intimate praise (never mind depictions of estrangement or disaffection), can and will offend. In 1996 I published a book of personal essays. My mother called to congratulate me. "Have you heard from anybody yet about the book?" she asked.

"Only my shrink," I joked. "He's upset that I've gone public with stories I should have only shared with him. He's threatening to sue me, Ma!"

"That's ridiculous," she's said, not joking, deadly serious. "If anyone's going to sue you over this book it's me."

But even if we never write about our families, there's still the often-painful fallout on our families from the dedication, time, and solitude that the art requires. I don't want to suggest, even for a moment, that artistic success depends on domestic instability or that there's any correlation between art and suffering. One doesn't have to have a tortured soul to become a writer. Or rather our souls don't have to be tortured any more than most people's souls are tortured. Catastrophe or self-destructiveness is no prerequisite for the position. Nor need one be a drunk, a womanizer, or a victim of abuse. If bad behavior or bad luck were an essential ingredient of a writing life, our detox centers, prisons, and twelve-step programs would be full of writers. All one has to do to be a writer is to write. We're writers only when we're writing. Writing, in other words, is an activity, it's something we do and not something we are. When we're not writing, each of us is just another poor slob trying to get through the day without hurting anyone too much.

That said, let's also recognize that many of us live within rather stringent economies of energy, and to do this is not to do that. With jobs, kids, relationships, it's impossible to balance the competing claims of life and art without slighting one in favor of the other. I should add too that the muse is an especially demanding and jealous mistress, and most of us when we're not writing wish we were. It may be that even if I were a shepherd or a proctologist, I'd be just as troubled as I've often been throughout my life, struggling to satisfy both my need to work and my need to love. Maybe, but I doubt it. The fact is, like most writers, I have been and continue to be monomaniacal about putting in my hours at the desk. And that dedication to work has sometimes proved lethal to my loves and friendships.

So the work itself always entails frustration and failure; it can damage our most intimate relationships; its public rewards are illusory at worst, fleeting at best. And if you write poetry, hardly anyone is listening. So why do it?

Elizabeth Bishop provides a possible answer in a famous letter to Anne Stevenson. Bishop writes that what we want from
great art is the same thing necessary for its creation, and that
is a self-forgetful, perfectly useless concentration. We write,
Bishop implies, for the same reason we read or look at paintings
or listen to music: for the total immersion of the experience,
the narrowing and intensification of focus to the right-here-
right-now, the deep joy of bringing the entire soul to bear upon
a single act of concentration. It is self-forgetful even if you are
writing about the self, because you yourself have disappeared
into the pleasure of making; your identity, the incessant tran-
sient noisy New York Stock Exchange of desires and commitments, ambitions, hopes, hates, appetites, and interests have
been obliterated by the rapture of complete attentiveness. In
that extended moment, opposites cohere: the mind feels and
the heart thinks, and receptivity's a form of fierce activity.
Quotidian distinctions between mind and body, self and other,
space and time, dissolve. Athletes know all about this nearly
hallucinatory state. They call it being "in the zone." They feel
simultaneously out of body and at one with body. I also think
that infants inhabit a rudimentary version of this state of
being. When my children were babies, I would often awaken in
the morning to the sound of my son or daughter babbling happily in the crib. They'd be talking, but the meaning of the words
was indistinguishable from the sensation of the sound, and the
sound was part and parcel of the mouth that made the sound, of
the hands and fingers that the mouth was sucking on as it sang.
No matter how sophisticated our poems may be, or how deadly
serious they are about eradicating or exposing the terrible
injustices around us, I still think that we are trying, by means
of words, of consciousness, to reawaken that preverbal joy, to

repossess, reinhabit, what someone else has called the seriousness of a child at play. Bishop says this concentration's useless
because it is its own reward, the mysterious joy of it. It is singing for the sake of singing. And even if the singing pleases others or consoles them, stirs them to further the cause of justice
in the world, or simply brings the parent to the crib with food,
warmth, and maybe a dry diaper, those effects and ramifications
are incidental to the primal, fundamental urge to sing, to the
sheer gaiety (to borrow a word from Yeats's "Lapis Lazuli") of
projecting our voices out into the ambient air.

Maybe it's because I do have ADD and have always been a
deeply and often painfully distracted human being, but my best
days are the ones when I sit down at the desk at 9:00 a.m., and
look up to discover that it's 3:00 p.m. and that six hours have
passed in a single moment. It doesn't matter ultimately whether
what I've written is any good or not. I always feel renewed
and grateful if the material, whatever it is, induces that self-
forgetful, perfectly useless concentration. While I'm working
I'm only working, nothing else exists. Inside and outside feel
perfectly aligned, and throughout the full range of my faculties
and sensibilities I'm entirely alert, entirely present, and this,
for me, too rare experience of being there, wholly there, never
fails to exhilarate. While it lasts, there's no joy like it. And it
never lasts long enough, or happens often enough to satisfy my
yearning for it. Dickinson describes its passing as a "sumptuous
destitution." Wallace Stevens expresses the desperate longing
to prolong this blessed state when he says in "Solitude among
Cataracts" that he wants to die in "a permanent realization."
The pleasure of that concentration is addictive, and it's that
addiction, I think, that accounts for the restlessness and mel-
ancholy many writers feel when they're not writing. It's not, as
Berryman believed, that poets need to suffer in order to write,

that misery produces art; it's rather that that self-forgetful, perfectly useless concentration makes them happy, is itself the happiness that may elude them or never come so purely or reliably in their nonwriting lives.

In February 2001, a month before Tim died, I flew to Chicago to spend a few last days with him. Tim was bedridden by then, his breathing labored, his consciousness a little compromised by lack of oxygen. One afternoon Reginald Gibbons, his good friend and editor at TriQuarterly Books, Reg's wife Cornelia Spelman, and I were sitting around Tim's bed, talking about poetry, as we almost always did. The subject of Tim's forthcoming book came up. He had just seen a mockup of the cover, which consisted of a picture of Tim fly-fishing, one of his great passions and the subject of many of the poems in the book. Tim was happy with the cover and hopeful that he'd be around when the book came out in the fall. I don't remember who suggested this, but Reg and I began to take turns reading from the last poem in the book, a poem in four sections called "Woodmanship." Tim by then was too weak to read out loud. His eyes were closed throughout the reading, while his fingers tapped out the rhythm of the poem on the bed's railing. Though fly-fishing is the occasion of the poem, the subject is really acceptance of mortality, failure, and loss, and the value of joy in all its elusiveness. Reg got to read the magnificent final section, in which the speaker fishes with a young boy he has befriended:

Early the next morning, I poach
In the Rod and Gun Club, the boy beside me,
In pitch black, making our way by starlight
And the cold flowing river.
We're being careful of sheriffs with sidearms,
I tell him, though an expensive tickct's about

The worst for getting caught these days.

In the preserve of the privileged, I whisper,

Honest men take small breaths to avoid

The smell of wasted, rotting game.

But poachers breathe

From the soles of their feet

The blue ribbon trout streams.

Now pine needles, now pungent, spongy sucking

Gives way to commotion: the slapping and thrashing

Of twenty-pound steelhead trout on the shallow gravel—

The bucks are biting each other's tails,

The hens are heavy with roe.

My heart aches.

Then finally, the long, moon-shimmering slick

Coming down hard into a sucking whirlpool.

In my desire it is already light.

The boy fishes: a crisp, short, roll cast—

And a huge steelie takes the lure deep in the hole.

The trout jerks its massively-jawed head once,

Then twice, as if trying to shake off a nightmare.

The boy strikes sideways, downstream,

To set the hook firmly.

I wait, calm, observant, almost indifferent now,

But still the old feeling comes—

Well being. Delight being. Joy being.

The sun breaking,

Birch branch shiny with spilled light

(Is it black on white

or white on black?)

The only difference now my knowing enough not to think.

Go joy. Fly.

I don't need you,

Which is why you've come,
Welcome back
My childhood's earliest familiar,
Omnipresent except when desired.
Still, if you will, take bread at my hand
Like any unsuspecting creature of the forest,
Eat the trail of crumbs I left to find my way back.
An explosion goes off in the whirlpool:
Silver with a rosy pink underbelly,
Predatory, unsuspecting, all of creation
Caught in its exquisite contortions,
A steelhead leaps—
The burden of the past and the future lifting—
Two feet out of the water
And throws the hook.
I move up beside the boy to praise his effort;
I try to comfort his unfathomable loss.

The poem, of course, is also about writing, the moment of creation, when we forget all else but the task at hand, when preparation and luck coincide, when the burden of the past and the future lifts, and exhilaration comes, what Tim calls delight being, joy being, his childhood's familiar. The poem itself, he implies, the writing of it, is both the crumbs that lead us as adults back to that childhood paradise and the measure of how far we've traveled from it. When the moment passes and the poem's written, and we rise from the desk to return to the world awaiting us, our tangled loves and commitments, the exhilaration is nearly indistinguishable from "unfathomable loss."

Career-wise, Tim's life was not a happy one. At the same time, in his last six years he remarried and had another child, and despite his worsening physical condition he did his finest writing. His life, in fact, contradicts the cliché that great art springs from misery. Illness and the terrors of dying certainly inform Tim's rueful, funny, heart-wrenching final poems, but so too do the joys of fatherhood and marriage, and the deep pleasure of domestic peace. The poems, in fact, are inconceivable without them. Ill as he was, in his last years Tim had never been so happy, as a writer or a man.

Early and late, though, Tim's only constant was his work, his poetry, the pleasure of sitting down to write each morning, and those marvelous days when hours would pass in what would feel like seconds. Through all the vagaries of love and loss, addiction, illness, and recovery, he took delight in the work, and the delight and the surprise that found him as he wrote these final poems are now our delight and surprise as we read them. It was for that pleasure that he wrote. It was for that self-forgetful, perfectly useless concentration that he kept on writing, even when the world paid no attention. He didn't write for fame, however much he may have longed for recognition and suffered keenly for the lack of it. He wrote for the sheer joy of the writing, which, as a writer, was his most durable sustenance. It was less than he deserved, but, lucky for us, it was enough to keep him going.

Acknowledgments

The author thanks the magazines and journals in which these essays, or some version of them, first appeared:

The Cincinnati Review: "Why Write?"
The Cortland Review: "Technique of Empathy: Free Indirect Style"
Literary Imagination: "Translation as 'Linguistic Hospitality'"
The Los Angeles Review of Books: "Convention and Self-Expression"
New England Review: "Mark Twain and the Creative Ambiguities of Expertise"
Virginia Quarterly Review: "My Tears See More Than My Eyes"
Tikkun: "Some Questions Concerning Art and Suffering"

"Why Write?" also appeared in *The Best American Essays*, ed. Lauren Slater, series ed. Robert Atwan (Boston: Houghton Mifflin Harcourt, 2006).

Much thanks to Tom, Michael, Charlie, Robert, Gaby, Daniel, and Reg for their help and inspiration. Great friends, even better readers. Thanks too to Randolph Petilos for all his indispensable work on the manuscript, for his keen eye and ear, and his incomparable generosity; and to Ruth Goring for her editorial expertise. I also need to thank the Bread Loaf Writers' Conference and Warren Wilson's low-residency MFA program, for which many of these essays were written.

Poems quoted in full are Philip Larkin's "High Windows" from *The Complete Poems of Philip Larkin*, edited by Archie Burnett, copyright © 2012 by The Estate of Philip Larkin, originally published in *High Windows* in 1974, reprinted by permission of Faber and Faber Ltd., and Farrar, Straus and Giroux, LLC; Dan Pagis's "Written in Pencil in the Sealed Railway-Car," copyright © Dan Pagis and ACUM, from *The Selected Poetry of Dan Pagis*, edited and translated by Stephen Mitchell, English translation copyright © 1989 by Stephen Mitchell, published by the University of California Press; Thom Gunn's "The Beautician," "Donahue's Sister," and "Slow Waker" from *Collected Poems*, copyright © 1994 by Thom Gunn, reprinted by permission of Faber and Fabert Ltd., and Farrar, Straus and Giroux, LLC; and Louise Glück's "A Fantasy" from *Ararat* (Ecco Press, 1990), reprinted by permission of Louise Glück.